TAKE TWO
AND CALL ME *in the* MORNING

TAKE TWO AND CALL ME *in the* MORNING

Prescriptions FOR A
Leadership Headache
—PAIN-FREE FOR 30 DAYS—

GERRY CZARNECKI

MILTON RAE
PRESS
NEW YORK

TAKE TWO AND CALL ME *in the* MORNING
Prescriptions FOR A *Leadership Headache*
—PAIN-FREE FOR 30 DAYS—

ISBN 978-1-61448-323-6 paperback
ISBN 978-1-61448-324-3 eBook
Library of Congress Control Number: 2012945356

MiltonRae Press
an imprint of
Morgan James Publishing
The Entrepreneurial Publisher
5 Penn Plaza, 23rd Floor,
New York City, New York 10001
(212) 655-5470 office • (516) 908-4496 fax
www.MorganJamesPublishing.com

Cover Design by:
Rachel Lopez
www.r2cdesign.com

Interior Design by:
Bonnie Bushman
bonnie@caboodlegraphics.com

In an effort to support local communities, raise awareness and funds, Morgan James Publishing donates a percentage of all book sales for the life of each book to Habitat for Humanity Peninsula and Greater Williamsburg.

Get involved today, visit
www.MorganJamesBuilds.com.

TABLE OF CONTENTS

INTRODUCTION

THIS BOOK IS A 30 DAY cure for the pain of leadership headaches. Yes, there is not a leader out there that has not felt the "pain of leadership headaches." Indeed, what you have here is a collection of messages that are offered as a prescription for those who find that leadership makes them feel sick, even debilitated. Being a leader is a challenge for everybody who ever wore the mantel of "boss." One of my books was titled, *Leadership… One Thing after another*, and that title probably feels familiar to anybody who finds themselves in a leadership role. Every day is a challenge, as we encounter issues that challenge our judgment and, at times, our patience.

In *Take 2…And Call Me in The Morning* we make reference to what so many have heard from doctors when called because we felt sick. I am obviously not a doctor, but I have been "doctoring" leaders for a long time, and the message in the title is, you do not need me to tell you what to do, you already know that. What you need is the confidence in what you already know: enough confidence to take the action in the face of uncertainty, and the lack of guidance on specific actions.

The guidance is also never perfect, and seldom will it cure anything. All it will do is give you comfort, even confidence, that some reasonable action is better than none. I try to give you a dose of the remedy for the pain and frustration every leader faces. Most of the day-to-day-circumstances you experience probably feel unusual, even unique, but the plain fact is that most, if not all, of these situations have been experienced by leaders for centuries. There is no way that any one book can create examples of all the potential issues that will arise on a day-to-day basis and this book is no exception. You are going to be challenged to generalize these ideas.

Although leaders do many tasks, as I have written in previous books, I believe that you can boil down the role of a leader into key principles. Each principle is a simple concept to explain but not always easy to accomplish. In previous books, I had the **LEADERSHIP** mnemonic, where each letter represents the essence of a key principle for peak performance. The leadership principles started with **L** for love, followed by **E** for expectations, **A** for assignment, **D** for development, **E** for evaluate, **R** for rewards, **S** for systems, **H** for humor, **I** for integrity, and **P** for passion.

For those who have not read my previous books, (a condition I hope you will remedy someday), I have reprinted the First and Last Chapters of my *Lead with Love* book as a bonus appendix to this book. Reading these will help a good deal to understand the underpinnings of my leadership messages to you. If you really want to get the whole story, then get ***Lead with Love***.

The first of the Chapters, *Love,* defines the core philosophical basis for your behavior in your role as a leader. The last Chapter defines the importance of *Passion* in the mind and heart of the leader. This is that intangible emotional commitment that drives the leader to act on principles, rather than the situational easy way out.

Our journey through this book will take us through these principles, but this time on a case by case basis, not integrated into the mnemonic. The structure here is prescriptive. I have outlined a 30 day period of learning. There is a section to be read each work day. I gave you the "weekend off," to reflect on what you learned and practiced during your workweek. These readings are short, yet loaded with experience. They include my years of experience leading and coaching, and the experience of many who came before you, with real life problems. Obviously I have changed the names to "protect the innocent," but the stories are real. Indeed, if you have been leading for any period of time, you will recognize many of the circumstances.

One caution, do not read this book in one sitting. That would be like taking a whole bottle of Aspirin at one time. I actually want you to take each section one day at a time. Let that message settle in; let the lesson get into your "blood stream" so that it can influence your thinking slowly, but surely. Learning in small does can give you time to think, and I want you to think. I want you to understand, and remember. My goal is to change you and your behavior, not just to get you to buy the book.

By the way, there is another bonus to this book. It is a personal "doctor house call" by giving you a free consultation that you can get any time you want. Just go to my Blog at <u>www.gerryczarnecki.com</u>, and ask your question. In return, I will tell you to "Take 2, and… and rather than call me in the morning," I will answer you in the morning, on the Blog, no call by you required. Doctors may have stopped house calls; but you can get your own "Leadership house call" from the Leadership Doctor.", by simply using the power of the web.

YOU

SELF — "LEADERS MUST LEAD THEMSELVES"

HOW MANY TIMES HAVE YOU gotten up in the morning, gone to work, returned and gone to bed not having a clue as to what you did that day? Many of us have had that happen and then passed it off as just another aspect of the daily grind. I can remember, early in my career, finding myself on such a treadmill. I was more or less adrift without any concept of where I was going.

When I took my first job, I got off to a rocket fast start. I managed to move up quickly from one job to the next, and was lucky several times to "be in the right place at the right time". My career took off, and with each new job I faced challenges of increasing intensity that took more and more time from the rest of my life. I did not complain, because I wanted to succeed. I also had the good fortune of an incredibly supportive wife who was successful and hard working on her own. She understood and shared in my desire for success. All of this fed a frenzy of activity, most of which I thought was good.

To be honest, I had no real idea where all of this work was leading me. I had spent virtually no time thinking through what I was doing in my career or where my career was going. As long as I was moving forward, with more and more challenges and responsibilities, there was no time or reason to think about me. I was consumed by the job, and for a very long time that was all that I needed.

After I had worked for about eight years, it finally dawned on me that I was doing nearly the same things that I had been doing at the start of my career. Yes, I was working in bigger organizations, had a bigger title and was making more money; but in many ways, what I had done in the past year was the same as what I had in the previous eight years. This realization was shocking, but also life-altering.

For the first time I realized that I was not in a "career", I was in a job; and that I was not necessarily doing what I wanted, I was doing what my boss needed and wanted me to do. Satisfying the needs and wants of a boss is in itself a bad thing. On the contrary, being the "go-to-person" has a great deal of merit, as was evidenced by my explosive rise in the hierarchy. The problem was that I was paying no regard to my needs, my career, and my future. That was when I started to focus on "Self."

Making my "self" a priority does not mean being selfish. I didn't reduce my efforts at work, or avoid the hard assignments; but I started to ask myself the "what about me?" kind of questions. Those questions lead to the conclusion that I needed to make some changes to achieve the vision I had for my future. In short, I started to realize that "self" was a priority in my life.

As I said earlier, making my self a priority was not "selfish". The distinction is that the self-focused person looks beyond what "is" and envisions what can and will be. This was the time when I really started to ask the question "How am I doing?" Although I had given and received many performance reviews over the years, I had never before thought to do one for myself.

The short version of the story is that I did my review and then spent a great deal of time deciding what I wanted to be at some time in the future. This process triggered a series of actions on my part, through which I was ultimately transformed into a very different person. I went back to school and took a large number of courses that would enhance my knowledge, skills and behaviors. I started focusing on outside activities that would establish my credibility in areas I needed to add to my portfolio. I read new and different books, attended new organizational meetings, joined some new service and professional clubs, and networked in all of them. In essence, I remade myself. At the end of about five years, I had the experience, credentials and contacts to be considered for a much different set of jobs. It took some time, but I got my career on the track that I wanted and I never looked back.

I lead myself to a new and fulfilling career. You can do the same by reviewing where you are, where you're headed, and where it is that you really want to be. Take the time to consider *your* SELF.

SECTION II: Mini Case — I Quit

Brent had been a supervisor at the same organization for 11 years. As the company's expert in automobile financing, he knew that he was respected for his expertise. Although he enjoyed that recognition, he felt unfulfilled in his job.

At home in the evening and on weekends, Brent would spend hours drawing and painting. He had discovered several years ago that he was a pretty good artist, and that it gave him great pleasure to create a painting that people would admire and enjoy. He wished that he could spend more time painting, but there were only so many hours left in the day after work.

Today, Brent went to work and something snapped. He realized that he was 38 years old and that he simply did not like his job. He liked the people, he liked the company, but his work just felt like a drain. Right after lunch, Brent went to his boss and quit. His boss was shocked, and frankly so was Brent.

Now What for Brent? – Brent probably did the right thing, but at the wrong time. He acted on impulse, and now he is facing no income and no plan for the future. If you are feeling like Brent, unfilled and drained by your job, please step back and give yourself a chance think the situation through and make plans. Becoming somebody or something else is a process, and it requires not only following your heart, but also creating a plan for the journey.

The first step is to love yourself. You should care enough to invest the time in thinking through where you want to be, and how to get there. Perhaps Brent has decided that painting is important to him and that it's what he wants to do. The problem is that the expression "starving artist" is not just an expression-- for many it is a reality. Brent is only focusing on his desire to paint, when what he needs to do is step back and rationally asses how he can fulfill all of his dreams and aspirations. With his artistic talent, it is possible that a career change to the advertising department would be both a practical solution and a fulfilling outlet for his creativity.

Maybe he should take a painting class to see just how much better he can get. If he has extraordinary talent, formal training could enable him to truly make a living from his art. Another option would be to stay with his current job and try selling his paintings "on the side." It could be that although painting is a great therapy for him, it is not something he should be doing full time. On the other hand, if he can become commercially successful, there will be plenty of time to shift his life in that direction.

I am not suggesting that Brent should stay in his job and remain miserable forever. He should consider his short- and long-term options, and develop a plan that will lead to where he really wants to be. Just walking away from that which he knows, and has been very good at, could be a disaster. Making the *right* move, not just *some* move, is what he--and you--should always aim to do.

SECTION III — The Doctor's Rx

Caring for the self is often precipitated (as in my case) by a realization that something is wrong with the status quo. Initially, the focus is on what's wrong. Ideally, you should start with a clear understanding of what you are doing, then assess what it is that is wrong, and finally, what courses of action might be available to you.

Being unhappy in a job does not always result from being in the wrong job; it often results from doing a job for the wrong person or in the wrong organization. If that is your case, explore all of the options, including a candid discussion with your boss. Many times, those conversations can spare you from making a radical move by dealing with the issue directly and effectively. Bosses often have no idea that they are in some respect problematic for the people working for them. A careful, but honest discussion can help clear the air and enable you and your boss to focus on improving the relationship.

At other times, a discussion that brings to light a discomfort with a job can lead to a quality reassignment, either within the same section or department, or elsewhere within the same firm.

I have not met many leaders who wanted to make their staff miserable. Most of us actually do know how to love; but even if your boss has not learned that core concept, he or she probably cares enough to try to help relieve your pain. Always give your boss the benefit of the doubt, and I think you will be pleasantly surprised.

SECTION IV — Ask the Doctor

Phil: I love my job, but I am going nowhere in pay. What can I do?

The Doctor: This is a short and simple question, regarding a complex issue that can rarely be resolved with a short and simple answer. On the one hand, you should consider yourself extremely fortunate that you love your job. On the other hand, you feel unfortunate in your pay. That could be a real problem, or a real *perception* problem.

While not everyone loves their job, most people are convinced that they don't make enough money. The question is whether you are being underpaid for your job, or if you are in a job that just doesn't pay well. For example, teachers often love their job; yet many of them leave teaching because they cannot make the money that they want. Although they may well deserve to earn more, teachers are paid according to a general salary range for that profession. The same is true for every job in every industry. This is not an economics lesson, but it is important to remember that the "laws of supply and demand" tend to set the value a society puts on workers. Many people in teaching love what they do, and do it in spite of the fact that they are not the highest paid people in their neighborhood.

On the other hand, if you are actually underpaid for the job you are doing, then you may have a problem that needs action. The first option is always to have that conversation with your boss. If that seems impossible, then maybe you need to "test the market" outside your company.

The other factor could be that your performance is not up to "Expectations." If not, and assuming you know if it is or not, then you need to work on your "self" to find a way to improve. If that is the case, your commitment to self will drive you to either get better trained, better focused on the key skills and knowledge necessary to get better, or you will ask the company to help. All of these are things you need to take ownership of. Do that, and you will have explored the possible alternative futures.

Do not stay in your current job if the pay is a problem that you simply cannot get out of your head. If you do, you will eventually become bitter and angry and then your performance will deteriorate and the pay situation will probably get worse.

2

DEVELOPMENT — "THE GOOD GET BETTER, THE BEST EXCEL!"

HOW MANY OF YOU WENT in to work this morning hoping that today everything would go perfectly? Your staff will be productive… there will be no errors, no complaints from the customers or the boss, and all work will be done on time on budget… there will not be a single personnel problem because the entire staff will be humming as a team. Such days are rare in any work environment, but they can and do happen. "Perfect days" happen when the team members are all working to achieve mutual goals and they are all excellent performers.

Most leaders have never experienced a perfect day. Indeed, many years ago, a cynical but probably all-too accurate friend of mine said that his definition of management was, "…one damn thing after another." I laughed when I first heard that, but every time I have used that expression with groups over the years, I get this knowing nod that clearly suggests that there is painful truth in the comment. Being "In Charge" means being responsible for a sequence of challenges that need resolution. In short, each day is spent going from one problem to another.

What can we do to make the transition from the status quo of endless problems to the productive hum of perfect days? Some would say: nothing. There is no chance to be in the "perfect world" because life is tough and unfair, and every job involves reckoning with reality. Others, and I include myself in that group, believe that (although perfection is probably never achievable) striving for perfection is a rational goal. Unfortunately, most of us do not strive for perfection; instead we settle for goals well short of that. A discussion on "striving to be the best" is a subject for another day, when I address continuous improvement as a core value for all leaders. Today's focus is on *helping your staff* constantly strive to be better.

Every leader must be committed to helping their associates to grow and improve. This requires a commitment not just to giving your staff the opportunity to achieve, but also to developing their capabilities. As leaders, we must commit a major part of our normal work day to helping our staff grow. We must teach, coach and support the growth of our associates. Anything less would be neglecting our core leadership responsibility. Development, the fourth word in our LEADERSHIP mnemonic, is a central concept in the journey towards being Leaders.

Developing staff is hard work. If you are developing staff, you are not going to go about your own work and enjoy a day of perfection. You are helping your staff to find mistakes, avoid mistakes or recover from mistakes. Your day can only get better, and come closer to that perfect day, if you are working with your staff to grow and improve. If you want a day where you can enjoy the pleasure of no problems, then you must invest in your staff so that they can develop their knowledge, skills and even attitudes that affect performance. Fail to invest in them and you will fail to reap the rewards of peak performance by your unit.

SECTION II — Mini Case - Leave Me Alone

Janet was into her third week of work as the supervisor of accounts receivable and she was having a tough time. Fran, her most senior clerk, was simply not responding to some feedback that Janet had given her last week. Janet had watched the error reports coming from the system and had found that Fran had the highest reject rate of any processing clerk in the section. In her feedback session last week, Janet told Fran what she had found and all she heard from Fran was, "Leave me alone, I have been doing this for seven years and I know what I am doing." Janet did not know what to say, so she just walked away.

This week, the quality reports from the system indicated that Fran's error and reject rates were even worse. Janet decided that she would talk to her boss about the problem and when she did, her boss told her that Fran has always had high reject rates, but that she always caught up on her backlog. He also added that she was a loyal and reliable employee who had great attendance and had stepped in when he needed help with overtime work. Janet asked her boss if Fran had ever been to the new formal training program on the accounting system and he said no. "In fact," he said, "Fran was asked to go about ten months ago and she refused, saying that she was too busy at the job to take the time off. I agreed with her that she was busy and told her we would work her into another session, but we never did find the time. You probably need to try to find a convenient time to get her to the training."

Janet went back to her desk and remained frustrated. Now she knew that she was not going to get much support from her boss, other than his agreement that Fran should go to the training.

Question: What should Janet do now?

The Doctor: This is not an uncommon situation, and unfortunately, the attitude expressed by Janet's boss is not unusual either. Janet really has only two choices: 1) Leave Fran alone and hope that she does not get any worse or 2) Work with Fran to help her understand and correct her problem.

Most leaders will take the first option, and assume that they are taking the lower-risk course of action. It could be the lower-risk choice for Janet, but that is assuming that she expects to be in this job for a short time, and that her current boss remains her boss during that time. I could not recommend that she follow that path, but we all know how tempting it is.

Option two is really the only correct scenario. It will be a challenge, and it comes with the risks that Fran will complain to Janet's boss at a minimum, and possibly even quit. Despite the risks, Janet must commit to helping develop Fran. It is essential for Fran to attend training; and if Janet can arrange it within the budget, she should eliminate the possibility for excuses by having someone take over Fran's work during the training period. Once she has been through training, it will be much easier for Fran to focus on the process she should be following and to ensure that she is using the system correctly.

There is no fast solution to this problem, especially given the position that Janet's boss has taken. Janet should go slowly, but she must proceed with efforts to help Fran grow. It is as essential for Fran's long-term development as it is for the well-being of the unit.

SECTION III — The Doctor's Rx

There is no easy way to get associates to commit to training unless the leader sets the pattern early. In the preceding case, Janet made the mistake of not acting immediately to get her associate trained. Most leaders have access to training programs for their staff. The smaller organizations may rely on "On the Job Training (OJT)" more than larger companies, but every organization has some process or resources for training new staff members. If you have formal training programs, then you should be firmly committed to sending all of your staff through those programs. You cannot allow the pressure of "getting the work out" to serve as an excuse to deny them, you and the unit of the knowledge and skills developed by training. When it's possible, new associates should attend training well before they take on a full work load in the unit. It is much easier to give them up during the time that training requires *before* you have become "addicted" to their output.

SECTION IV — Ask The Doctor

Paige: I have been the supervisor of my unit for two years and I have never been trained. What should I do?

The Doctor: It is a sad reality that many supervisors have not been trained in the technical aspects of their job; but the more serious problem is the lack of leadership training. I cannot tell from your question, but assuming that you have not been trained in either aspect, the following is my suggestion to you: Start by asking your boss if they have any training in the organization that would be helpful to you. My guess is that there is training of some type, but that you were not assigned to participate because your boss had the thought "I can't have her go to training because I need her here and there's no one to step in and supervise her section". If you get a response like that from your boss, then I suggest that you go to HR and ask them what training is available. You can then go back to your boss with a request to go to a specific program, and make it easy on him or her by proposing a plan for covering your work unit while you are gone.

If that does not work, then you are going to need to create your own development plan that will enable you to grow on your own. Some activities for you to consider include attending seminars or other courses, finding a mentor, and reading books that will help you to improve and learn. It may not seem fair, but it is essential for you to take responsibility for your own growth. I will talk more about this in an upcoming issue of the newsletter, so stayed tuned!

Ted: I have been working with a really weak associate for more than a year now to try to boost his performance, but he just isn't responding. I'm wondering what I should do at this point?

The Doctor: Make certain that you have tried a variety of ways to assist his development. Sometimes we continue teaching or coaching somebody precisely the same way, over and over again, even when they do not get it. I have found that as a teacher or coach, it is essential that I try different approaches because not every one learns in the same way. Try using different examples, different times of the day or perhaps having somebody else do the coaching. It is possible that a new approach will be exactly what your associate needs.

If you can honestly say that you have tried all of the reasonable approaches, and that there is still no improvement, then it may be time to have a counseling session with your associate. Although it's difficult, it may be time to say, "I'm sorry, but I do not think this is the right job for you." You may be very surprised to find that he already knows that, and you are simply voicing his own frustration. If that is the case, then the two of you can work on solving problem, perhaps he is better suited for another job in your unit, or a different unit in your organization. There are times when you truly cannot help somebody improve. That is not defeat or failure on your part, it is simply reality and you owe it to your associate, yourself and your organization to deal with the mismatch.

3

Time to Look Back in Order to See Forward

The world of work is not specifically tied to the calendar year, yet we are part of a culture in which the turn of the clock on the last day of the calendar year signals a "New Year." The whole world seems to celebrate the start of the new year, and most businesses have their "annual results" measured on a calendar year basis. The "end of the year", as we artificially define the period, actually does have real value to us as leaders. By having the measurement period defined at the same time each 365 days, we have the chance to reflect on what we have done, and how we did. It is clearly the time for evaluating both our own performance and that of others.

Most leaders do, and should, evaluate the performance of the organization on a variety of parameters. We look at the goals, both quantitative and qualitative, and attempt to determine how well the organization did. Part of this evaluation is the "ritual" of doing year end performance appraisals on our staff. Irrespective of the merit of a single "annual review" most merit compensation systems are tied to the year end evaluation, and almost all incentive pay systems are tied to the year end results achieved.

Unfortunately, many leaders neglect to do their own evaluation. There will eventually be a "performance appraisal" from the boss or bosses, but seldom do leaders take the time to write an appraisal of their own performance. A candid self critique is the most useful, and probably the most difficult, evaluation that the leader will ever get. No evaluation from a boss can replace an honest personal self evaluation. Unfortunately, most leaders have great difficulty in doing a candid self appraisal because defense mechanisms assist the leader in rationalizing the impact of mistakes and failures.

Leaders must be able to be truly objective about their own performances in that role. The leader must decide on each parameter of leadership, hopefully using my LEADERSHIP model, and then objectively evaluate personal performance against those criteria. That is no small task, but the truly great leaders do it regularly, not just once a year.

Once the committed leader evaluates what has taken place in the past, the next step is to plan the future. This is not a business plan, but rather a "Leadership Plan". No leader is perfect, and no leader can ignore the need for continuous improvement. Last year you made leadership mistakes that were errors of commission or omission, but there were errors. Make certain that you dig deep inside yourself to see both, and then develop a plan to improve. This is not a New Year's resolution, it is a plan. You must lay out goals, strategies and action plans for change, as well as deadlines for the accomplishment of those goals. This leadership plan may only be seen by you and your conscience, but it is even more important than the business plan that your boss and your staff will see. This plan will be your guide to being better able to help those who work for you to achieve not only their goals, but the goals of the organization.

SECTION II: Mini Case —
Ralph the Disappointed Leader

Ralph has been the Director of Marketing for his company for five years and until this last year, he was on "a roll." For four years running, he had constructed plans that his team executed and did them magnificently. The marketing results for the company were well beyond those of the competition, and the growth in sales volumes was leading the company to superior performance by any measure. This year, however, was very different and Ralph knows that his team has let the company down.

The staff had experienced significant turnover the previous year, resulting in a team that was less qualified and even less focused on the goals. Ralph had been on the road almost non-stop most of the year, so the staff was often working without his supervision. Unfortunately, they had not performed well and Ralph was clearly unhappy. It was clear that Ralph's boss was unhappy with the situation as well. The pressure towards the end of the year had grown very intense, and Ralph knew that the pressure was only going to escalate in the coming year.

The business plan for next year has been "put to bed" and his team knows that the numbers are a major stretch and leave no room for error. Ralph has very little confidence that they will be able to meet the goals. He is convinced that they simply do not have enough experience, know enough about the company or actually care enough about the goals to achieve success. He is heading into the new year with a feeling of dread that it will be another year of failure.

What can/should Ralph do?

Ralph appears to have accepted little or no responsibility for the failure of his team. Four years of success probably caused Ralph to become overly confident about his own abilities. It sounds like he is setting the goals for his staff (along with his boss) but that he is not engaging them in the process. In addition, he does not seem to understand that turnover is both a problem that could be a reflection of his leadership, and a problem that could create the failure to perform.

He seems to be aware of the fact that his people may not have the right skills, experience and attitude; but he is missing the point that this is his responsibility, not theirs. Ralph clearly appears to have a leadership problem, and hopefully he will do his own evaluation and come to the same conclusion. It is pretty obvious that previous employees left him for reasons that may have to do with the fact that he was not in the office much and therefore, not available for nurturing and guidance.

As a practical matter, Ralph needs to have a preliminary session with his staff; then a diagnostic with each member to determine what they need in the way of Development efforts. It is critical that Ralph take an honest look at his own leadership activities and determine what he needs to do in order to be the effective, proactive leader he had been during the first four years. It is not unusual for leaders to fall into the trap of thinking that once they succeed, that success will continue to happen. Every day must be a point of renewal and re-energizing. That is why, at a minimum, the best leaders use the annual "New Year" to critique themselves and identify where they can improve, or fix their own behaviors. Your staff looks to you for guidance and example, so show them your commitment to improving at the same time that you set out the ways in which they can improve.

SECTION III — The Doctor's Rx

The greatest tip for any leader is to remember the humility we all need to be truly successful leaders. Self reflection at any time of the year is useful; at the end of the year we have an opportunity to candidly evaluate ourselves and to make adjustments. Some of the questions you should ask:

1. Did I achieve my personal goals?
2. Did we achieve the organizational goals?
3. Is my staff achieving to maximum of their abilities?
4. What have I done to help the staff get better?
5. What more can I do to help them?
6. Have I been a good boss? A bad one? What makes me what I am?
7. If I lost people from the staff during the year, why? Did they leave for the reasons they said, or did they leave because I failed them?
8. Where is the quality of the staff less than what I need to have the organization achieve excellence?
9. Does the staff truly understand what I expect of them? Do they have expectations of me that I am not fulfilling?
10. Are there staff members who should not remain? What have I done to help them with their failures? What have I done to reward their successes?
11. Does the staff get adequate training from me? Do they need formal training from outside our organization? What have I done to assure their continued understanding of the opportunities in the company?
12. Do I spend enough time with the staff? Have I answered questions effectively? Have I been there when they needed me?

13. Have I rewarded excellence, or simply rewarded a mediocre performance? Do I punish too much?
14. Do I love the staff, or do I simply like them? Do I serve as a role model for their behaviors? Do they enjoy working for me? Would I work for me?
15. What do I need to do to be a better boss, a better leader?

SECTION IV — Ask the Doctor

Tony: I have done all of the things that you recommend, I have asked all those questions and believe that I am doing everything right. Even so, and I still keep coming up short of my own expectations. What am I doing wrong?

The-Doctor: Tony, with such a short question, I have no idea, but I suspect that one of two things is true: either you have expectations that are unrealistically high, or you have not been honest with yourself about your performance as a leader.

In the first case, you could be striving for a goal that is unattainable and hence, you are being disappointed by falling short. I used to teach a Capstone Course on Business Strategy in the MBA program at a major university and many of those students truly expected that within five years they were going to be the CEO of a company. They had their expectations set so high that there was an almost 100% chance that they would not achieve their goal. I met many of them years later and they often asked me what went wrong. I tell them that nothing but their expectations went wrong. One or two might have actually achieved that goal, but it was almost invariably because those people started their own businesses. The average MBA graduate is simply not going to be the CEO of a company five years after achieving the degree. That is an unrealistic expectation, and if they continued to cling to that fantasy, they would clearly be falling short.

If you are not setting wildly unrealistic goals, another possibility is that you are infected with the fatal flaw of hubris. In doing your self evaluation, you may conclude that you are doing everything correctly, when in fact, you are blind to your own faults. It is not unusual for strong people to have a tough time seeing their own weaknesses. There is a fine line between self confidence and arrogance. Arrogance can lead to overlooking the weaknesses that we all have. If you think you are doing everything right, you probably are not.

I suggest that you experiment with a 360 degree evaluation. In your case you need to ask your staff what they think. I know that may be tough for you, but a tough evaluation from your staff might shed light on your shortcomings. In addition, you probably received feedback from your boss, and if you are a victim of the hubris disease, it is likely that you have already rejected that feedback. Nothing could be a more serious mistake than to ignore feedback from your boss, unless it is feedback from your staff.

If your staff has a view of you that is completely out of sync with your own, then you must reconcile the two. If the view of your staff is coincident with that of your boss, then you have a very serious problem. The problem could be that they are both wrong, but unfortunately, it is most likely that they are correct and that you have closed your mind to the truth. Whatever the case, the truth must be determined if you are ever going to improve your leadership.

4

FIND YOUR FUNNY BONE

SUCCESSFUL LEADERS TAKE THEIR jobs seriously; but successful leaders don't have to be so serious on the job as to be somber. Work is not a laughing matter, but leaders should find ways to incorporate laughter into the workplace. Studies have shown that humor plays an important role in a healthy work climate. In the current business environment, stress and well-being are recognized as factors that impact an individual's productivity and success. The benefits of humor as a means to diffuse tension and relieve stress should not be ignored.

The benefits of laughter include reducing the level of stress hormones and increasing the health-enhancing hormones such as endorphins and neurotransmitters. It provides a physical and emotional release, a distraction from negative emotions such as anger or stress and it enables us to see challenges from a different perspective. Laughter is contagious: it elevates the mood of those around us and creates a positive social interaction. Whether one associate is having a bad day, or a team of associates is facing a difficult situation at work, laughter will temporarily divert attention away from the problem. The diversion will likely improve their ability to cope with the challenge.

Humor in the workplace involves some risk. By incorporating humor, you lighten the tone of the work environment. If this is taken too far, it can spin out of control and result in reduced focus and productivity. Humor also has the risk of falling flat or being offensive. Humor in the workplace is not about telling jokes, and should absolutely not involve off-color or politically incorrect statements or behavior. Humor in the workplace can be as simple as keeping a smile on your face, or cheering up an employee with a kind act and supportive words. If an associate is having a bad day, get a couple sugary treats from the snack machine, then go to that person and say "I wanted to sweeten your day" and offer the chocolate bar and candy.

There are countless ways to lighten the mood or cause a laugh, and you don't have to be a funny person to incorporate this element into your leadership role. Don't try to be a comedian if it's not your style; furthermore, the humor should not cross the line from what is appropriate in a professional environment. Your office is not a comedy club. It is a place where your associates should feel that it is fun to work. In many respects using humor is simply behaving in a way that is humane: be supportive, nurturing and caring.

SECTION II: Mini Case — Barbara's Bad Day

Barbara works as a senior reporter for a local newspaper in a large city. The reporters and editors usually meet first thing in the morning to discuss the latest local developments, brainstorm on story ideas, and receive their daily reporting assignments. This morning the meeting was scheduled for earlier than usual due to an increase in the volume of news as a result of upcoming elections and a recent storm that had caused a lot of local damage. As a features writer for human interest stories, Barbara would be responsible for interviewing some victims of the storm who were suffering from damage to their homes and the loss of power at their businesses.

When she was about to leave for work, her 12 year old son David announced that he was sick and planning to stay home from school. She talked with him and realized that he wasn't ill; he wanted to stay home in order to avoid a test in math class. After 45 minutes of cajoling and threatening, she was able to drop David off and head to the office. Getting such a late start meant that she was stuck in the worst of rush hour traffic, and she arrived at the newsroom well after the morning meeting had concluded. Barbara was a highly regarded reporter and conscientious employee, so it was upsetting for her to have personal issues affect her professional life. Furthermore, she knew she would have several new assignments for the day and would be under even more pressure to meet her deadlines.

She went directly to Jim, the managing editor, to apologize and find out what she had missed in the meeting. Jim was very understanding as he had worked with Barbara for several years and knew that she would not be late without a legitimate reason. He reassured her that he was sympathetic and had faced similar challenges with his own children. They discussed her assignments, and then Barbara went to her desk to begin making calls for interviews and checking facts for two of the stories that had been assigned to her. The newsroom was designed for the reporters, editors and graphics team to openly interact, so Jim was able to see and hear what happened next.

Barbara began checking the facts that an intern had researched for her story, and realized that there were several errors and inconsistencies. This meant that she would have to spend even more time redoing the research herself. She called the intern over to her desk and reprimanded him in a way that was clearly humiliating to the young man. Ten minutes later, a woman she had planned to profile for a storm-related human interest piece called to say that she didn't want the public attention and was backing out of the interview. Barbara was frantic, knowing that she would have to start from scratch on both of these stories and therefore have to stay very late to finish her work. She thought of her son coming home from school to an empty house and started to feel as though she would break down in tears if her day continued like this. She simply couldn't handle the weight of her responsibilities and the pressure. Her head began to pound and she couldn't even focus on what to do next.

From across the room, Jim observed Barbara deteriorate under the stress. He knew from experience that Barbara was strong and capable, but that she was human. He also knew that she became grumpy when she went too long without a solid meal. Based on her late arrival, he guessed that she had not had time for breakfast. Jim made a quick decision and went downstairs to the deli on the first floor of the building. He glanced around for a snack that would boost her energy and saw something that he thought might boost her spirits as well.

Upon returning to the office, Jim walked over to Barbara and when he had her attention he pulled a lemon out of his pocket and put it on her desk.

"Barbara, this day has been a real lemon for you. I'm sorry that it has been so rough, but you need to start over." With that, Jim pulled a lemonade out of a bag and set that on her desk. Despite herself, Barbara started to laugh. It was either that or cry, and it was such a welcome relief to break the tension by laughing. She realized that the world wouldn't come to an end over one bad day. After sharing a laugh with her, Jim then handed over a bag with chips and a sandwich and kindly insisted that she take her lemonade and food to the lunch room and come back to her desk after she was nourished and ready to make a fresh start on the day.

The Doctor: When life hands your associates lemons, a loving leader will make the lemonade.

We all try to organize our personal and professional lives so that they run smoothly and don't negatively affect one another. Inevitably there will be times when family will take precedence and interfere with our plans at work. There are also times when work demands that a personal plan is sacrificed or put on hold. A loving boss recognizes that an associate's happiness and productivity involves more than what goes on at work. In Barbara's case, she was a valued and reliable employee who was simply having a bad day. Rather than reprimand her or make her feel worse about her predicament, Jim eased her tension through humor. If he had not given her a chance to restart her day, he faced the risk that she would lower others' morale by communicating poorly with them the way she had the intern. By helping Barbara, he also helped the people who would be interacting with her.

Making lemonade out of lemons is an old saying that Jim turned into a physical act of humor and kindness. Humor can take many forms, but the goal is to evoke pleasant feelings through unexpected or exaggerated acts of encouragement. Jim demonstrated that he is truly a loving boss and a leader who employs humor to lighten the mood and assist his associates in being healthy and productive.

SECTION III — The Doctor's Rx

I do not consider myself funny and I'm not good at telling jokes; I do have a sense of humor, and enjoy others who have a quick wit. My career has been in a traditional corporate environment in which professional and businesslike behavior set the tone.

Despite all of this, I have found ways to incorporate humor at work:

- Set the example for your staff. Smile, laugh, be upbeat and friendly.
- Take every opportunity you can to find humor in the day-to-day events. Find humor in travail, find humor success.
- Have brainstorming sessions in which funny, wacky and crazy ideas are encouraged.
- Recognize when stress levels have reached a high and call a time out. Take the staff to lunch, order in a pizza, send everyone outside for some fresh air – anything that will be a pleasant diversion.
- Humor involves elements of surprise, exaggeration and fun. Think of ways to surprise your staff and encourage them to enjoy the moment.
- Seek out humor in your own life so that you feel comfortable when it's time to lighten up and elicit a laugh.

SECTION IV — Ask the Doctor

Brad: In my previous job, I was very successful as a client representative at an ad agency. A bigger, rival agency recently recruited me to be the senior vice president, which was a great step up for me in my career. I am now in charge of 20 associates who work in all aspects of the advertising business: copywriting, creative, art design, graphics and sales. My team seems really capable and motivated, but I am uncomfortable with the work environment. My boss, who is the owner of the agency, is a very serious, bottom-line kind of man. I am much more light-hearted and prefer to incorporate humor and sometimes zaniness into the workplace to stimulate creative thinking and the exchange of ideas. This was the environment at my old job, and we came up with some really fantastic ad campaigns when we were joking around and bouncing crazy ideas off each other. My new boss has criticized my efforts to lighten up the office culture. He recently told me that I needed to focus the staff on getting the work out and that my levity was just distracting them. I don't know what to do. I am happy to have moved forward in my career, but this job is starting to feel like a big step back in my happiness and ability to succeed.

The Doctor: I am an advocate of humor in the workplace because it is proven to relieve stress and enhance productivity. However, "humor" does not mean constantly telling jokes or having a free-for-all environment. Humor should not interfere with one's ability to accomplish work, it should improve it. In your case, I agree that humor fuels creativity-- which is critical in your field of work. You describe yourself as "light-hearted" and in theory I think that is an appropriate manner to encourage open communication and creativity. If your associates feel comfortable with you, they are much more likely to speak up and share their crazy ideas, one of which might be a brilliant idea. However, if your boss feels that your humor is preventing the team from doing their work, it may be that you have taken humor beyond what is appropriate in a professional environment.

Another possibility is that you and your boss are not a good match. A person's sense of humor, or openness to humor, is an important consideration when interviewing. The tone of an interview is typically serious because this is a time to present a very professional image on both sides; however, it is also important to consider whether the person will "lighten up" outside of this setting.

My recommendation is that you go to your boss and have an open discussion about the role of humor in your office. Explain that you think it is important to stimulate the creative process.

Then ask him what aspects of your behavior he thinks need to be adjusted in order for the team to work effectively. A good compromise would be to schedule a half hour daily session in which the team can exchange ideas and act "zany" and then return to more focused and disciplined behavior.

SPRING HAS SPRUNG...
WHAT NOW?

MY LEADERSHIP AND STRATEGY consulting, as well as board governance activities, keep me on airplanes a great deal throughout the year. In a two-week period, I may be in 10 different cities and airports, allowing me to witness how the seasons affect people in a variety of regions and climates.

In most of North America, the end of winter elicits a sense of relief that the cold and weather-related inconveniences have passed, and that the reawakening of spring has brought with it a fresh start. "Spring fever" has almost always meant a desire to be outdoors and enjoy the freedom that good weather offers; but "spring cleaning" has always meant that with the passing of the dirty (sometimes dismal) season comes the need to clean the house until it too is fresh. In many ways, these two rites of the season can serve as a metaphor for us as well: it's time for spring fever to refresh our minds and spring cleaning to refresh our goals.

Although I do not propose that focusing on the "Self" should be a single annual event, the renewal aspect of spring makes it an appropriate time for us to go through the process of leading ourselves. We all know the feeling of being so busy that we forget or neglect to make time for self-reflection and assessment. Have you spent time recently to reflect and assess where you stand on your life plans and goals? Regardless of today's date please put yourself in a season of renewal frame-of-mind and take the time to focus on you.

As leaders who truly want to help our associates achieve success, we must constantly give of ourselves to our associates, but we may deny ourselves the focus of our own leadership. The tragedy of such a mistake is that when we let ourselves down, ultimately we will let down our associates as well. If we do not love ourselves, set expectations for ourselves, make certain we are assigned properly, pay attention to our own development, evaluate our own achievements and then reward our successes… our ability to grow and sustain success will diminish and eventually we will stagnate. In short, the principles in the LEADERSHIP mnemonic must be applied to ourselves as well as to our associates.

Personal stagnation does not just hurt us; it also hurts those we are attempting to lead. If we cannot achieve our goals and continue to grow in our careers (and in our personal growth goals as well) we will eventually become incapable of being the leader of our associates.

There are at least two reasons for which our own stagnation will result in our failure to lead. The first of these reasons is mostly personal…if we neglect our personal and professional development, we will be unable to support the growth of those who look to us for leadership. As others continue to evolve but we do not, our leadership will diminish to the point where either our staff will look to others for that leadership, or our bosses will look to others to move the organization forward.

The second reason is the more serious leadership disaster. If we fall behind in our own development, some or all of our staff will achieve less success than they had the potential to achieve. If you truly agree with the proposition (that I set forth in my book and this newsletter) that it is the leaders' responsibility to develop and facilitate the success of our associates, then this is a much greater tragedy for us and the organization. In short, we owe our staff to stay at the "top of our game." If we do, then we will be better able to make certain that they stay at the "top of their game."

If you really believe that it is your responsibility as a leader to help others succeed, then you must do the spring cleaning on yourself. Make certain that you still have stretch goals. Make certain that you are in a job that both matches your skills and challenges you to grow. Look at your own development plans and make certain that you have not slipped in your resolve to take the next step in your formal education, or perhaps finish your next degree. Look at your performance on the job and assure yourself that you have not fallen into the path of least resistance, rather than constantly seeking to improve your performance. And lastly, make certain that you reward your professional successes with the opportunity to fulfill those desires to enrich either your own life, or that of the people most important to you. Finally, remember that all the gifts you have from your hard work can do wonders to help some of those who have been less fortunate and faced serious life tragedies.

SECTION II: Mini Case — Lost in Translation

Mini has been with the company for ten years and she is very proud of her conviction that the company recognizes her as an excellent leader. She has given of herself to all of her associates, and more promotions have been given to her staff than any other supervisor's in the entire company. Mini is clearly known as the best developer of leadership talent in the organization, and whenever the company hires a potential star, that person is invariably assigned to Mini.

Yesterday, Mini had an exciting meeting with her boss, Theresa. Their company was about to post a job opening that she, Theresa, was optimistic that she could get. Obviously, Mini was ecstatic because she was confident that if Theresa got the job that she, Mini, would be the perfect candidate to move up. After the meeting, Mini went back to her office and planned her strategy for taking over Theresa's job. That night Mini updated her resume/biographical profile and then listed all of the accomplishments that she thought qualified her for the promotion.

She worked all evening on the project, and by 10 PM she was finished with her effort. As she sat before the computer screen with the documents completed, she then started to write out on a piece of paper all of the names of the people she thought would be candidates for the job. When she had finished the list, which was just four names long, she then tried to objectively evaluate the strengths and weaknesses of each of the people. This part of the project to a great deal longer than she expected, but she also did a similar list on herself. By midnight, Mini was finished and she felt comfort in her analysis that she was at least as well qualified as the other candidates, and better in at least two of the cases. Mini went to sleep feeling pretty good about her chances.

This morning, she decided to talk to Theresa again about the job. Theresa told her that she thought that the job would be posted in about two weeks and that it would be about another four weeks before the decision was made. Mini then asked Theresa for a job description of her job and whatever qualifications that the company had placed as requirements for the position. Theresa gave her the specs for the job and the required qualifications at the end of the work day, so Mini took them home to read.

Reading the materials that Theresa had given her, Mini was stunned to learn that the requirements for Theresa's job include having a Bachelors degree with a major in accounting or at least fifteen years of accounting experience. Although she had a Bachelors degree, Mini did not major in accounting, nor did she satisfy the experience requirement. Mini was devastated to learn that according to the terms of the minimum requirements, she would be considered as a candidate for Theresa's job. Her dreams crashed before her, and Mini cried herself to sleep.

Issue: So what happened? Is there an error here, and if so, who made the mistake? What can you learn from this?

The Doctor's Comments: Theresa let Mini down. It must have been clear to Theresa that Mini had her eyes on Her job. We can only assume that Theresa never told Mini of the minimum requirements and that fact that she did not meet them. On the other hand, Mini failed to watch out for Mini. This is a classic case of leaving too much to your mentor, coach and boss. Everybody makes mistakes, and every once in a while, the best intentioned boss simply fails to help and to facilitate development. If Mini really wanted that job, she should have known that she needed to pursue her options: take courses at night; focus on another job; go to another company; or simply wait for the extra five years before she decided to thirst for the promotion.

This scenario happens far too often in organizations. Protect yourself by always knowing the parameters, which are sometimes not obvious. Be prepared to manage your own career and never delegate that to another, even if your boss thinks you "walk on water."

SECTION III — The Doctor's Rx

This tip really exists as part of the Mini case. The process that Mini went through in assessing her candidacy for promotion has merit, but it should not be held off for the day that a dream job becomes available. Work up that list frequently, know who the players are and make certain that you are not plotting against people. This process is "competitive analysis," and you should leave yourself plenty of time to fix the short-falls. In Mini's case, she needed to determine whether she would rather take courses at night or wait until she had accrued 15 years of experience. The lesson is that you should set your goals and plan to do the work required to achieve them, especially if it means development programs that take long periods of time.

SECTION IV — Ask the Doctor

Winston: I am a product manager at a consumer products company. I have been in my job for about five years and it feels like it is about time for me to move up or move on. I work incredibly long hours, and I am paid very well, but I have much higher ambitions and I just feel like I am not moving very fast. I talked to my boss and he told me that he knows that I am very good at what I do, but every time that he proposes me for a job, his boss says I need more time to develop. I have watched several product managers move to bigger jobs, so I am getting a little worried, what should I do?

The Doctor: Winston, I think you may have some good reason to worry. I have no idea what your performance appraisals say, but I assume you do. If you have not looked at them recently, you should ask to see your personnel file in order to determine what needs improvement.

It is essential for you to know the criteria for advancement. It may be that you are just being impatient; or it may be that you have a "hole" in your resume. Taking an inventory of the training, performance and even academic credentials of the people who were promoted may give you a better understanding of what it takes to move up in your company. Product management is often a pressure cooker job, with high risk and high reward. Maybe you simply have not done a good enough job to demonstrate that you are ready for greater challenges.

Another possibility is that you fall short in that mystical thing called "degrees." Many companies in your industry have a strong bias towards people with an MBA, and if you do not have one, it could be holding you back from advancing in your company.

Going back to school is often viewed as too time-consuming and painful, but I assure you, there are very few jobs in this era that will not require a major amount of renewal and additional learning. Our ever-changing society is not going to slow down the day that you "finish" school and enter the workforce. The pace of change will run away from you if you do not continue to grow your knowledge base. It is often said today that we need to renew our knowledge of our specific discipline every ten years. Many companies are sending their stars (even those who have prestigious MBAs) back to special programs that are offered on University campuses for professionals to renew their knowledge.

If the lack of a degree is holding you back, then you need to make a decision about your ambition. If your goal is faster growth, then you may need to make a commitment to a degree program. Either that, or look for a job with requirements that match your degree. Regardless of your decision today, keep in mind that ten years from now you may need to go back to school again, just to keep up with the increasing knowledge.

P.S. This advice is important to Winston, and it is even more important to those who work in technical fields. Science and technology, and even accounting and the law, are specific fields that are rapidly changing and require you to be continuously growing. You need to read professional journals on a daily basis, and keep your knowledge current. The expansion of knowledge may not be expanding as fast as computer chip technology changes, but fall behind in the newest developments and you may be left completely lost in just a few years.

Do You Have a Mentor?

THROUGHOUT MY CAREER, I have had mentors who have taught me valuable lessons, helped me make tough decisions and guided my efforts to achieve superior results. My successes would likely not have happened without the aid of their wisdom and support. Some of my mentors were my superiors, and others were my peers and personal friends. Each one of them has had an impact on my career, and their advice has stayed with me over time, providing continual guidance. I have also been a mentor to many individuals, who range from young people starting their careers to seasoned professionals, in need of an advisor to help them reach the next level in their goals. Having mentors and being a mentor are both wonderfully gratifying experiences.

My journey in leadership began early in my business career, at which time I found an incredible mentor to guide me. Gail Melick inspired me with warmth, discipline and an unwavering commitment to excellence. He was the most influential person in my professional development, and the impact of his mentoring has continued throughout my life.

Many of us go to our spouses or family members for advice. While they can be great sounding boards, they also have inherent personal biases as a result of the relationship. I consider my wife to be incredibly astute, and her opinion has positively influenced my business decisions. However, I recognize that our relationship is personal, not professional, and for the health of our marriage, I should leave the majority of my work-related issues at the office. Furthermore, I don't want my marriage to suffer if I don't always agree with her opinion or take her advice in regards to my business.

On the other hand, many times, her "first cut, gut reactions" have been right on target. Consequently, I frequently mention issues to her, even if at times, I think she will not really know enough to be on target. The irony is, she is far more correct than she is wrong. There is a lesson in that, sometimes knowing too much can be worse than knowing too little. We tend to get lost in the details, and forget the "overarching issues."

In contrast to close friends and family, a mentor is neutral and will give you the unbiased, unvarnished truth. Regardless of whether your business is currently running smoothly, or you feel that your performance needs improvement, you need to have someone you can turn to for sound advice. A recent article in *Business Week* told the story of a husband and wife team who were planning to start their own business, and sink their life savings into the endeavor. Despite having relevant experience, a great product and what they thought were well-crafted plans, when they asked for a loan, their banker advised them to revamp their business plan. The couple hired a consultant who had 30 years of experience in their industry. He was able to ask questions and address pitfalls that the two had never considered. Thanks to their mentor, the couple changed their business model and was able to open a retail store that has been a huge success.

The benefits of having an experienced professional guide you in your professional endeavors are countless. It can help you avoid costly mistakes, as well as devise better strategies for success. Your actions may be on course for achieving goals, but with the aid of a mentor who has been there and done that, you can increase efficiency and achieve superior results. In my current role as a mentor and consultant, I work with organizations and individuals to help them get past hurdles and continue to raise the bar on their goals and achievements. The desire for continual improvement is present in most of us, but we often need help to figure out how to do it.

More than a year ago, I was contacted by the CEO of a medium-size services company. He explained that while the company was by definition "successful", it was stagnant. He wanted to grow, move in some new directions, and achieve bigger goals. The problem was that the other members of the corporate team had very differing views about how the company could achieve growth with success, and the climate in the entire organization had become uneasy and contentious. I was hired as a consultant for the organization and as a mentor for the CEO so that he had a sounding board and advisor outside of his associates.

I started my work with them by conducting confidential interviews with each member of the mid and senior level management. Among my findings were that the company's culture had been negatively impacted by poor communication and fear of change. It was also apparent that a few individuals were not a good fit in their leadership roles. After working with the management on making appropriate changes and restructuring, the climate was restored to one of enthusiasm and team spirit.

In the next phase, we worked on strategy and opportunities for growth. My perspective from outside the organization enabled me to bring fresh ideas and strategies that management hadn't considered. It was also an advantage that my presence was neutral and therefore didn't pose a threat or the clash of opinions that had previously hindered management. While my initial engagement was supposed to be for a few months, they have retained me for more than a year now, thanks to the positive impact that it has had on their business culture and growth.

Mentors, also called coaches, have the ability to see and hear things that those who are on the "inside" may not be able to sense. Someone who isn't connected to the day-to-day operations has a different perspective and can therefore be an extremely effective advisor. Your mentor should be someone you can trust as a confidant who has expertise in your field of work or business. The role of a mentor is not to solve your insurmountable business problems, it is to help you navigate through the minefield, assist you to continually improve and guide you to greatness. If you don't have a person like that in your life, you need to find one.

SECTION II: Mini Case — A Side Order of Support

Jackie and her husband Stan had always loved to cook, and with three children to feed, making big family dinners was a pleasant ritual that they shared. As their children grew older and their tastes changed, including their youngest deciding that she was a vegetarian, the couple experimented with more exotic flavors and cuisine from a wide variety of cultures. Their love of good food even resulted in two family trips to Europe so that they could taste genuine French and Italian cuisine.

When her kids all left for college, Jackie truly suffered from the empty nest syndrome. Her daily activities had been focused on her children, their activities, and making meals for her family.

Cooking for two didn't seem nearly as fun, and it wasn't as challenging as pleasing the temperamental tastes of her children. Stan had it easier, as he had a busy practice as a dentist and his routine had stayed the same as when the children had been home. However, he was sensitive to his wife's situation and was concerned that she might have developed a mild case of depression. It was a great relief when Jackie told him with boundless enthusiasm that she had found "the answer".

Jackie had spoken to her old friend Joan who lived in another state. Joan was raving about a night out with her girlfriends when they had gone to a food assembly class and come home with 12 prepared meals that they could freeze and serve later. Loving the idea, Jackie did some research and learned that this was a not new trend and that it was a franchise concept that had not yet reached her town. The opportunity to own her own business that involved her passion for cooking seemed to be the perfect solution for her new phase in life. With some help from her husband and a loan from the bank, Jackie moved forward with her plans to open a meal assembly store in her town and one in the neighboring town. The franchise company provided the business plan and essentially everything that she needed to get started.

Now, with both stores open for the last five months, Jackie regrets the day that she spoke to Joan and launched her business. The business is not running smoothly, she is exhausted from driving back and forth between the two stores, and her employees are a constant source of headaches. Jackie has come to realize that while she was a "manager" of her children and household, she really doesn't know how to manage a business or staff. She knows that she needs help or the business will fail. The problem is that she doesn't have the financial resources to hire a manager or a professional consultant who could teach her and the staff how to make the business a success. Jackie is even more depressed than before, and she desperately wants to avoid being a failure.

Does Jackie Have Any Chance For Success?

Yes, if she gets the help that she already recognizes she needs. As somebody who has been the owner of a franchising company, and who is also currently the owner of a business that operates franchised retail stores, I understand the challenges that she faces. First, her staff has very likely not had any real training, and as a new leader, Jackie doesn't have the skills to train them herself. Second, Jackie needs her own leadership training, as well as a mentor who can guide her.

Firstly, the franchise company should be providing her with substantive support, and she needs to lean on them for help. There are actually many affordable programs and resources for small business owners to get the training and guidance that they need. There are a number of organizations that have created networks of retired professionals in a wide variety of fields that provide free consulting. There are also mentoring clubs where non-competing business owners meet to share experiences and offer advice and support. Another option is to seek out a low-cost consulting solution. Like many consultants, I offer phone and online consultations, as well as staff training, at discounted rates for small businesses.

The best chance Jackie has is to reach out for help. If entrepreneurs and small business owners all had to run their businesses without any assistance, there would be very few success stories. The key is to learn from others who have been successful in a similar endeavor. My final piece of advice for Jackie is to read my books You're In Charge…What Now? and Lead with Love. These books are ideal for a small business owner to learn the core principles of leadership and how to apply them to lead a staff to success.

SECTION III — The Doctor's Rx

In recent years, the industry of business coaching and consulting has grown enormously. There is an endless sea of coaches and mentors, and not all are alike. While it is exciting that so many people are willing to help, it is important that you find a mentor who is a good match. The two of you need to be compatible, communicate easily, and have a foundation of trust and respect. Here are some qualities to look for in a mentor:

- A good listener. Mentors can have a lot of good advice, but they have to listen to you for their opinion to be based on your unique situation
- Many years of experience and success in the same industry or profession
- A positive, upbeat attitude that will lift your spirits
- A calm nature and strong shoulders that will ease your fears when you think the sky is falling
- A realistic point of view and good common sense
- A perfect match may not exist, and you shouldn't wait forever to find the ideal
- Individuals with different backgrounds, talents and approaches may see things that you don't

SECTION IV — Ask the Doctor

From Gina: I'm the Executive Director of a local chapter of a national non-profit organization. We have a large board of directors with diverse backgrounds, professions and talents. Some of the board members are long-timers and others have just recently joined us. Throughout the past year, I have been frustrated with the board because they disagree and come to a stalemate on many issues, fail to implement actions that we were able to agree upon, and attend meetings sporadically so that no one ever seems informed and up-to-date. My small staff is over-worked as it is, and it seems that the board is more hindrance than help to us. How can I be diplomatic, and yet turn the situation around?

The Doctor: Your problem is unfortunately fairly common in non-profit organizations. It's good that your board members are diverse because it allows you to draw on a variety of talents and experiences, as well as represent the diversity of the community you serve. However, such differences can lead to conflict and hinder what should be a united effort. All of your board members are committed to the organization for personal reasons, and your goal is to have them work together in a professional manner. They need to understand their roles and responsibilities, which include attending meetings and respecting the opinions of others.

My recommendation is that you ask the board to attend a nonprofit training workshop. There are wonderful trainers and programs that specifically target nonprofit boards.

Indeed, I consider this issue such a challenge, that several years ago I was the co-founder of the National Leadership Institute for the purpose of providing affordable training for nonprofit leadership, and also wrote the book <u>You're a Non-Profit Director...What Now?</u> to supplement the workshops we provide. This organization is an excellent resource for those who work in the non-profit sector.

A "BOOK COVER" STORY— BE PREPARED TO BE SURPRISED

A TRULY EYE-OPENING EXPERIENCE occurred a few years ago when I was on my way from my home in Florida to Washington DC where I was going to conduct a seminar on Corporate Governance for 50 folks who are members and Chairs of Audit Committees on corporate boards of directors. I do many of these seminars each year, and I truly enjoy these opportunities to help board members become better leaders.

This trip was slightly different than usual because the airplane was full of people from South Florida who were fleeing before the appearance of hurricane Wilma; hence, the plane was full. I travel a great deal, and when I travel from Fort Lauderdale airport to DC I used to take a direct flight on Ted (United's former discount version of an airline) which had just one class of service. On these flights I always booked an exit row, aisle seat because it had significantly more leg room.

Thanks to my frequent flyer status at United, I was able to pre-board my flight to DC and was therefore comfortably settled in my seat when the majority of passengers started to board the plane. The seat next to me was not yet occupied, and obviously I was hoping that it would stay that way. Unfortunately, because the flight was likely to be full, I realized that an empty seat was not likely. I could only hope that my seat mate was not too large a person, because then I might have some shoulder room to go along with the expanded leg room.

As the plane filled up, and the candidates for my seat mate were fewer and fewer, I saw a very tall, at least six-foot-six young, black and athletic, muscular looking young man begin to walk down the aisle. I looked at him and realized that, because of the extra leg room, this man was going to be sitting next to me.

I was not mistaken and as he approached, this obvious "jock" motioned that he needed to get into the middle seat in my row. Now, my fate was decided. Just looking at him I could tell that this "tall drink of water" was a professional basketball player and would easily take up half my seat with his broad shoulders. Also, I have a pretty strong image of most basketball players being spoiled brats, so I suspected that he would be pushy and arrogant about how he needed to have plenty of room and was important enough that he might even try to "con-me" out of my aisle seat. I had a two-and-a-half hour flight ahead of me and began to prepare myself for a modestly unpleasant experience.

The man sat down, and immediately settled in, not really saying a word to me. He pulled out a newspaper and started reading while he tried to get comfortable. I realized that at least he was not going to be pushy, so I relaxed and opened my *Wall Street Journal*. I quickly got to the second page of the first section and began to read an article about how Google had managed to achieve a seven-fold increase in earnings in the last quarter. I am particularly sensitive to articles about Google because I am a bit of a technology "geek." I love technology and consider myself well-informed on the latest advances, and am usually one of the first to adopt the newest technology available to business. I also am interested in Google because when it announced its IPO (Initial Public Offering) I decided to pass on the opportunity to buy their stock because I thought it was greatly overpriced. Obviously that level of conservative investing cost me a great deal of potential profits because Google has risen in price dramatically since that IPO.

I was no more than three sentences into the article when my "jock" seat mate said, "Those guys did it again. I made a lot of money on that IPO. One of the best trades I made. Do you think that they will make their library deal work?" Ironically, I never flinched, and replied, "No, I think that they are going to be fought every step of the way by the publishing community and that they will not get a chance to ignore the copyright laws." He then replied, "I agree, I think that they will be stopped as well."

A few minutes later I was on to another page and an article about RIM (Research in Motion), the makers of the Blackberry. This time my seat mate said, "I think that those guys are in big trouble and I wish that they would just settle that suit because if they lose it, they are going have trouble surviving." At that point, I told him I agreed and we then proceeded to spend the next forty minutes talking about any number of companies and how they were doing.

I read a lot, and have a voracious appetite for business news. Furthermore, I do a great deal of strategy consulting so I spend enormous amounts of time keeping ahead of the news in the world of business. I also am an investor, and am pretty knowledgeable about a broad range of companies. The man next to me on the plane pushed my knowledge, and before we finished talking I was convinced that he had an edge on me. I was frankly blown away. This man was exceptionally smart and informed, very pleasant and a real gentleman. During our conversation I learned that he is a systems designer for a Florida company, a Florida State graduate in Computer Sciences, and an active day trader and a real estate investor who just finished selling three condos in South Florida for a very handsome profit. Ironically, I did get one thing right-- he was a junior college basketball player. But he quit playing ball when he became convinced that his coach was an idiot, and he decided to focus on classes instead. In short, my initial impressions of this man were totally wrong.

I am almost always a silent seat mate, because I usually use the time on the plane to work. I liked this man so much that I spent nearly the entire flight talking to him. He was a great conversationalist and a delightful human being. In short, I misread him completely, and I have not stopped thinking about it since I left that airplane.

I saw a tall, athletic looking black man and the stereotype of a basketball player came to my mind. This is particularly disturbing to me because since the time when I was very young (back in the early days of Martin Luther King) I have been a very active protagonist in the efforts to free the minority community from bigotry and bias. I am a bit of a civil rights crusader, but even I had formed a stereotype which influenced my perception of this man. I could not have been more wrong.

Look in the mirror. How many times have you looked at a candidate for a job and "judged the book by its cover?" I am a professional who prides himself on being able to select talent, and yet I made a terrible, stereotypical judgment while in the casual environment of an airplane. When you meet and interview candidates for jobs, you must challenge yourself to avoid bias and stereotyping. Do not let first impressions influence your goal to get to know the candidate, as those initial impressions may be based on a stereotype. Aim to get inside the heart and soul of the candidate by asking questions and listening to responses. Follow-up with further inquiry, but pay attention to what you are hearing, not just what you see. You may be pleased to discover a hidden diamond within that candidate.

SECTION II: Mini Case — Please Notice Me

Jan is a supervisor in the document section of a law firm. She has been there for seven years and is known in the firm as a very reliable employee. She is responsible for six clerks who maintain the huge number of document files for this 100 partner law firm. Although they have become highly automated, the hard copy files remain a primary component of the firm's files.

Jan has been working hard to do a great job, and she has also been focused on moving ahead in her career. During the last seven years, she has completed her bachelor's degree, become certified as a paralegal and took law school classes at night. She has just finished her first year in law school and she is now three years away from achieving her goal of becoming a lawyer.

No one in the firm knows about Jan's ambition. Jan is modest about her achievements and has only revealed that she is "taking a few courses at night". The only person who knows that these courses are toward a degree from law school is her best friend outside the office. The partners in the firm still don't even know that Jan has an undergraduate degree.

Last week, Jan learned that there was a paralegal opening in the firm and she decided to apply for the job because it would give her some experience in preparing documents and working with the attorney group. When she submitted her application, her boss said that they already had three experienced candidates who were being interviewed and that she would probably not be an acceptable candidate. At that point, Jan finally spoke up and said that she had gotten a paralegal certificate and was really hoping that she could make the move to use her training. Unfortunately, her boss said that they needed her right where she was and that just having a certificate would not qualify her for the job.

What should Jan do?

Jan must learn to do a better job of explaining not just who she is and what she wants to do, but what she has already done. It is a great tragedy in corporate (or professional) America that many who aspire are not recognized. This is a classic case of that tragedy. Here is a woman who has finished an undergraduate degree, completed paralegal training, and—most importantly—gotten into law school and completed the first year. She did all of this while working her nine-to-five job. She is a budding star and should be given every opportunity to grow in this firm.

Jan's achievements demonstrate her capability, but she needs to gain self confidence. She is accomplishing things that should give her the "power" to enhance her own career. She should have told the firm about each accomplishment as it was achieved. Just getting the degree was a huge step, getting accepted to law school was phenomenal and successfully completing the first year is something that the firm should be supporting.

If she actually did all that, and the firm still did not recognize her accomplishments, I would advise her to either focus on getting the degree and then leaving, or to start looking immediately. My first impression is that this firm is not able to see past the cover and does not deserve her.

SECTION III — The Doctor's Rx

It is critical for leaders to not make the mistake I made in judging the young man on the plane or that the law firm made in ignoring Jan. As leaders we must always be look past the superficial cover and find the "star" within. Jan is a star within. Somebody in that firm should know enough about Jan to have learned of her ambition and the fact that she was actively and successfully pursuing it. Every boss needs to "get to know" the staff.

Getting to know them does not mean intruding in their personal lives. It means understanding and caring about the things that are important to them. Learn what interests them, what motivates them, what they want to be "when they grow up."

Being friends can be bad for bosses, but being friendly and interested is good. We must allow ourselves to know the people who work for us, and the only way we can really get to that stage is to be "human" with them. Having a cup of coffee with a staff member or a group of them does not need to create friendship, but it can establish an emotional bond that will help the "Jans" of the workplace reveal their goals and ambitions. As bosses, one of our great opportunities (and responsibilities) is to help the staff realize their dreams.

SECTION IV — Ask the Doctor

Sylvia: I am a bank teller and have been for five years. I graduated from high school with highest honors and planned to go to college right out of school, but my father and mother died in an auto accident and I had nobody to take care of me, so I went to work immediately after graduating from high school. Now, five years later, I really want to go get my degree and become an accountant. What can I do?

The Doctor: Sylvia, I am sorry to hear about your great loss and I am proud of you for getting hold of your life and surviving.

I am also delighted that you want to go back to school! Start by taking courses toward the degree, and begin planning how you are going to get work experience that complements what you want to do.

If your bank has a tuition assistance program, then be certain to take advantage of that aid. It would be a great help to you in covering the cost of tuition, and it will let your employers know that you are working to further your education and career. Unlike Jan, do not keep it a secret. Make certain your boss and others at the bank know what you are doing. You do not need to brag, but should not be shy about the fact that you are working to improve yourself.

Find a way to get into the controlling or accounting department quickly, as it will enable you to do work that is directly related to your education, and you will be with people who will understand and appreciate your growing knowledge of accounting. They need qualified accountants and if they do not support your goals for advancement, then you need to know that right now.

If your company is as insensitive as Jan's firm, then do not stay one minute longer than it takes to find one that is and one that will help you pay for the degree. The smart ones will and there is no reason to work for a firm if it is not committed to your development. If all they are doing is judging you by your "current cover" then they might not be smart enough to know how valuable you can be when you grow.

DAY **8**

WHAT'S NEXT IN
YOUR CAREER?

LAST MONTH I ANSWERED a question from a reader who was concerned about how his performance appraisal might influence his career ambitions. That is really only half of the question he should be asking. Career advancement is determined not only by what we do at work today, but also what we will be able to do tomorrow.

It is true that effective achievement in your current job is an important factor in getting the next job. In the "real world," promotions are almost always based on of your performance. Most bosses view their best performers as the ones who should be considered for promotion, so in order to be in that pool of candidates, you need to be an outstanding performer. Seldom does a boss recommend a poor performer for promotion, so the first rule of getting ahead is to do your job well.

If you are a success in your current job, it is still no guarantee that you will be promoted, or that you would succeed in the position above you. In my book, <u>You're In Charge…What Now?</u> I stress that when leaders pick people for promotion they must not be confused by how well somebody does in their current job, but rather, how well they are suited to the new job. Leaders often make the mistake of picking their best performers and promoting them to jobs that they simply cannot do. A typical example of this is when superior individual performers are promoted to be supervisors, and it turns out that they have no real capacity to lead. When offered a promotion, it is critical to consider whether you have the knowledge, skills, attitudes, behaviors, and desire to succeed in the new job. If not, then your promotion will make you transform from a solid achiever in the old job into an unsatisfactory performer in the new job.

When you imagine your future, what type of job do you want to be doing? Is it something that you want because everybody tells you that it is the way to get ahead, or is it something that you really think you would enjoy doing and that you have the skills to do well? Far too many great salesmen become sales managers only to find out that they do not like the job and are not very good at being in charge of a bunch of independent people just like themselves. Success at one type of job is no guarantee of success at another, even though there are many who would tell you that a winner is a winner is a winner, no matter what the job.

It is probably true that there are some people who can succeed in nearly any job that they are asked to do, but those people are an exception. You may be one of them, and if so, then you are blessed with a unique talent. For the rest of us, we need to evaluate what it is that we do well, and that for which we are not suited. When I started my career, my graduate degree was in Economics and I had a pretty solid understanding of how business worked. I decided that if I was going to be a great banker, I needed to have a better understanding of accounting. While I was working, I went to night school to study accounting, ultimately took the CPA exam and passed.

I learned a great deal, and being a CPA has turned out to be a very useful credential for my career; however, I also learned that I am not cut out to be an accountant. I can do the work, but I would not enjoy doing it every minute of my working day. Indeed, I also discovered that my attention to detail is just not strong enough to be certain that I would avoid mistakes that could cause problems for the firm or the clients. I learned that I liked leading professional accountants, but was not a great accountant myself. I am convinced that had I tried to be a professional accountant in a public accounting firm, I would never have made partner because I would have been a mediocre accountant at best and the promotion criteria for partner had to include professional excellence.

Are you great at what you are currently doing? Does that matter for the next "logical" promotion? Are you ready for the next step up the ladder? Will your boss think of you as being ready simply because you are great at what you are doing? It is essential for you to make a judgment about what is best for you and your abilities. If you are doing a great job currently, your boss is likely to think that you should be promoted. If you know that the promotion would be a mistake, will you have the strength to not take it? If you believe in your ability to take on the next job, then aspiring to it will be a worthwhile goal.

This leads to the real issue: what are you doing to prepare for your next job? The key to that answer is in your personal awareness of what it takes to be well prepared, and your willingness to do whatever is necessary to be ready when the time comes to be considered. Seldom will your career advance based on the learning you had when you started. In the fast-moving world in which most of us work, yesterday's learning may be far short of what is needed tomorrow. Continuous, lifelong learning is essential for us all. If you are to be ready for tomorrow's job, you need tomorrow's knowledge and skills. Attitude may be a necessary aspect of your success profile, it is also not sufficient.

Decide what you like to do, evaluate what you are good at, then set goals for additional learning and improvement in the knowledge and skills required to move to the next level. Do not assume that doing a great job today will be sufficient to get you there, but remember that it is usually a condition for being considered. The smart boss will also look at your potential and your ability to fit the requirements of the job. If you want to be a successful candidate, make certain you know those job characteristics and that you do everything to match your "personal package" with the requirements.

SECTION II: Mini Case — Carolyn the Lawyer

Carolyn is a Harvard Law School graduate who has been practicing law for a major law firm for the last seven years. She has proven to be a great SEC practice attorney who has prepared hundreds of documents in support of initial public offerings. Her competence has parlayed into strong relationships with many of the clients whose companies she took public, and she has become the general counsel for several of them. Yesterday, one of them invited her to join his organization full time as an Executive Vice President for Administration. This job would mean a huge increase in the breadth and scope of her activities, as the CEO wants her to take on virtually everything except finance and manufacturing.

Carolyn had previously considered leaving the practice of law, but decided that she really likes what she is doing and knows that she is good at it. This new position would be a dramatic shift from what she currently does; and she would have a huge impact on the firm. Her client has told her that if she does really well at the job, there is no reason why she could not eventually run the company. That prospect got her attention. The thought of being a CEO was something that she had never really considered, but the opportunity to become the first female CEO in their industry was really tempting.

Carolyn knows that she needs some advice, but there is really nobody in the firm with whom she can discuss the situation. That evening she talked with her best friend Julie, who told her, "Carolyn, you would have to be crazy to take that job." Carolyn was shocked. "Why are you being so negative about this phenomenal chance to grow?" she asked Julie. "I know these people, I know the company and I have great respect for the CEO. Why would I turn it down?" Julie thought for a minute and said, "Because, it is a terrible job for you. There is nothing in that job that you will enjoy doing. I simply cannot see you managing the Human Resources function, or worse yet, worrying about the drivers of the delivery vans, or the maintenance staff in the building, or the purchasing staff." Carolyn heard that and answered, "Well, I would not be supervising those people, they would be managed by others." Julie said, "Yes, but ultimately, it would be your responsibility and you would need to focus on those issues every day." Carolyn was upset and conflicted, and went home to spend the rest of the night trying to decide what to so.

Question: Should Carolyn take the job?

This situation and dilemma are common among professionals. Carolyn has a very difficult decision to make. The real issue was identified by Julie: would Carolyn enjoy the job? She has been working in an area of great sophistication and complex legal issues. The new job sounds like it is very important to the company, but it is far from legally sophisticated. On the other hand, how can Carolyn ignore the opportunity to become CEO some day?

We do not know enough about Carolyn's skills, nor do we know how she would actually react to the new types of duties; but we do know that she would be taking a dramatic turn in her career. My guess is that Carolyn should not take the job. The promise of being a CEO might tempt her, indeed it might tempt me, but if many aspects of the work would bore her, and if she is not somebody who really wants to be a leader, she will not be a good fit in this role. Her chances of failure are pretty high, and I would not bet on her happiness in that job. If she is not happy, then she is less likely to be successful.

SECTION III — The Doctor's Rx

Are you ready for the "next job?" This is a question you should be asking yourself on a regular basis. You should not be preoccupied with the question, but you need to have an answer. If the answer is yes, then it is generally a matter of waiting for the right opportunity, or even actively looking for it. If the answer is no, then you need to define the aspects of you and your knowledge, skills attitudes and behaviors that will prevent you from being considered, let alone being a successful candidate.

Make a list of where you fall short, and then review that list, asking yourself: Can I make these go away? Can I actually increase my ability to be "qualified"? What do I need to do to either improve or change my behaviors? What knowledge do I need to gain? What skills or credentials do I need to close the gap between what I am today, and what I need to be tomorrow?

The most important result of this process will be your honest assessment of your ability or interest in pursuing the factors that will qualify you. If those factors are outside your comfort zone, or are something you simply do not want to commit to, then you probably need to abandon that position objective, and create a new set of goals.

If on the other hand, you decide that you can do those things, then you need to put together a plan to add those competencies to your resume. Then, the real test: do you have the discipline to follow the plan and to accomplish the metamorphosis? If you do have that discipline, then you will achieve your goals and you will probably get the job.

SECTION IV — Ask the Doctor

Calvin: I am a forty-three-year-old machinist working in a custom metal working shop making specialty parts for the automobile industry in the "rust belt." I have been doing the same job for almost 25 years and I am bored. Furthermore, I know I should be more optimistic, but the US auto industry has performed so miserably in the last years that the future looks really bleak for people in jobs like mine. I have always worked in this industry, so I don't know what to do.

The Doctor: There are many people in your industry who are facing the same tough questions. Some jobs, some companies, some industries are simply not the "place to be" in these tough economic times. It is a real dilemma to be in your position.

There is no simple solution, but it is essential that you start making a plan right now. It will not be easy, but you need to develop options for the future. Indeed, your firm is probably under severe strain and you are simply reflecting their collective anxiety. My advice is to apply the self-evaluation and development process that I described above, but recognize that your task may be take longer than for someone just hoping to be promoted. You might need to develop a new job skill set; perhaps you will need to change jobs, and maybe even relocate to another city or state.

When people with industrial age skills like yours are faced with the prospect of firms in their industry disappearing, it is often necessary for them to completely reinvent themselves. This can be daunting, but if you do not take action on your own, some day you may wake up and find that you have no job and no prospect for a new one. Now is not too soon for you to start planning the rest of your life.

Week 2

THEM

DAY **9**

EXPECTATIONS

"SETTING THE BAR Sets the Tone"

Can you imagine playing the game of American football, without knowing the rules of the game? From the name, you would assume that the game is primarily about a ball that comes into contact with the foot. If you were sent out on the field without the rules and without ever having watched a game, your expectation might be that you were to kick the ball past all those people and take it to the other end of the field. Well, if you were in Europe, that might be the case, but the game would probably be soccer, which is actually called "football" in French, Spanish, Italian and German.

Sports are often used as metaphors for our experiences, and in this example the metaphor demonstrates that the name of the game can often be misleading. The only way to play the game properly is to know the rules, and to understand the expectations-- which may be that you should somehow get the ball over the goal line, but <u>not</u> by kicking it. Unfortunately, all too often in the world of work, people are put into jobs and are given far too little guidance as to what the expectations are, hence they really do not know what or where the goal is. This is where every leader must start...You must define what the expectations are for the <u>unit</u> and for every <u>job</u> in the unit. Without expectations, how can your staff know when they have achieved success?

The importance of expectations seems obvious, yet far too many leaders do not focus enough attention on this crucial first step in leading. The key to setting expectations is that they must be clear and specific, so that every associate assigned to that job understands them and is held accountable for them. It is impossible to hold your associates accountable if they do not know what is expected of them; it is also impossible to hold them accountable if you have no way of objectively determining if the expectations were achieved. Every expectation must be measurable, which provides you and your unit with an objective assessment of success and failure.

Much has been written about goal setting, and even more has been written about how the goals get established. It is not our objective here to sell one process or another. There are those who believe that goals that are set mutually by the associate, and therefore "owned by the associate" are far better than those that are mandated by the boss. Others believe that clarity, understanding and acceptance of the expectations are the essential elements that make for effective goal setting. Whatever the management style or philosophy, it is clear that without expectations being set, your staff will flounder. In that situation, you and your unit's performance will flounder as well. You must, in whatever way works for you and your associates, make certain that every job, and eventually every person in those jobs, clearly have expectations that guide the work.

SECTION II: Mini Case — A Successful Failure

Brian has been a sales representative at an auto parts manufacturer for the past seven years, and has consistently received great performance appraisals from every boss that he has had. Two years ago, Sally took over as his boss, and since then Brian has been very uncomfortable in his job. Sally has rarely spoken to him on a one-on-one basis, and has seldom checked on what he's doing on the job. They only meet occasionally, and it's usually at trade shows or at quarterly national sales meetings where they hardly have a chance to talk. Although Sally hasn't communicated it to Brian, he is certain that she is unhappy with his work. He just doesn't know why.

Having pleased all of his previous bosses, and having increased his sales each year (this year was no exception!) Brian expects that Sally is also satisfied with his performance. He asked some of the others in the sales force about their sales numbers, and determined that his own numbers were about in the middle of the pack, certainly not in the lower fifty percent. Given these results, Brain was convinced that he was doing a good job, and that the problem with Sally must be some kind of misunderstanding. He tried several times to talk to her about it, but Sally was always too busy for a real discussion. All she had said to Brian was that he should continue to do what he was doing, and to make certain he kept sales growing. Most of the time she would add something like, "Let's make certain we get together the next time we are both in the same place at the same time." Unfortunately, the timing never seemed to be right.

From Sally's perspective, Brian is one of the old timers who fail to understand that mediocrity is not sufficient for success. She has some really ambitious sales goals, and Brian's numbers are far below what she needs from him if she is to achieve those goals. Sally knows that customers really like Brian, and that her predecessor had been very high on his performance, so she is puzzled by the fact that he is falling short for her. She has nothing against him, and would like to sort out what it is that is holding him back, but she just never has the chance to spend any serious time with him. Her own boss expects her to be making calls on all of the major customers, which takes her out of the office over 70% of the time, and the other 30% is almost always spent catching up on sales reports and senior management meetings. Sally is very concerned about Brian's sales and she has been talking to her boss about the fact that she needs to hire some new staff who can take over the key accounts that Brian and a few others from his era are handling. She is eager to move out the non-performers, and to build her team with star sales people. It was clear to her that Brain would have to go.

Question: Is Sally a good leader?

The quick answer is a resounding no, and the reason is simple…If Sally ever set the sales expectations for Brian, he certainly does not remember them. We cannot be certain, but it seems that Sally has done a terrible job of communicating her expectations to Brian. It is also quite clear that unless Brian really has a serious memory deficiency, he is working in a vacuum where he believes he is a success, although admittedly not a star. Sally's view is entirely differently, as she sees Brian as a failure. Hence we really have a "Successful Failure." There is a complete "disconnect" between Sally's expectations and Brian's understanding of them. Obviously, it is the leader's responsibility to ensure that expectations are understood, so there is no way to let Sally off the hook.

There is another problem in this case, and it is fairly common in sales organizations. The tendency to have a sales force traveling a great deal, and to be geographically disbursed, results in members of sales teams having very little personal or one-on-one contact with their leaders. This situation means that every opportunity for communication must be used to the greatest benefit. Sally needs to plan interactions with her team and with each individual, and must also use each incidental meeting to reinforce her expectations of the individuals and the unit. Being close to the customers is admirable, but being invisible to your staff is unacceptable.

SECTION III — The Doctor's Rx

It is essential that every leader focus on setting expectations, and setting them at a level that is both challenging and reasonable. "Stretch goals" are great for helping organizations achieve peak performance, but if they are so difficult that they become "impossible dreams" in the minds of the staff, they are no longer stretch goals, they are frustration generators. You must work hard to determine what is truly in the realm of possibility. It may be great to have one of those "Big Hairy Audacious Goals" (BHAG) but if they are so audacious that they cannot possibly be achieved, then they will be disregarded. (Note: If you are not familiar with BHAG, I highly recommend that you read the outstanding leadership book *Built to Last: Successful Habits of Visionary Companies* by James C. Collins and Jerry I. Porras.)

In determining goals, you should look at the historical data, evaluate what was done in the past and who did it. Choose a few of the stars in your unit and test your ideas on them. If they think that the goal is far too "stretch", then you can be certain that the others will resist even giving it a try. The opinions of the top performers are critical in a unit. The staff is usually aware of the stars, so if you can get them on board many of the others will follow. If you fail to get the support of yours stars, it will kill the effort with the rest of the staff.

Setting the bar at the right level requires creating some "pain." If the staff can coast to victory, then that is what they will do. If they need to push themselves, then the great people will do that and you will find a new standard of performance. Sometimes the expectations will be mandated from above, and if so, you must embrace these goals and communicate them to your staff. When it is your turn to set the expectations, make an honest assessment of what will be a reasonable stretch for your team, and then inform them of the goals.

SECTION IV — Ask The Doctor

Iris: I have one staff member who refuses to accept the goals of the unit and his share of responsibility in achieving those goals. His argument is that he has been with the company for twenty years, and therefore knows that the goals are unrealistic. I checked with some other units, and their goals are very similar to ours.

The Doctor: If you have seen other units in the company achieve goals similar to yours, you should feel confident in the expectations that you have set for your unit. In your case, you have an "old timer" who believes he is better than your staff, in fact probably you as well. You cannot let this continue. There is no doubt that a one-on-one meeting must happen soon.

In that meeting, you need to first listen to the explanations for his behavior. He may actually have some insights that will help you to understand him. He may also show his ignorance on a material piece of information. Whatever the case, you need to then work him through the logic of the goals. Understanding is an essential first step which he needs to take if you are going to get him to accept the expectations. Do not expect that one session will solve the problem. He has been around a long time and his opinions have been formed and cemented into his behavior. It will take time for him to embrace your goals. Be patient, but not weak. Give him time to see the light, but do not let him ignore it forever. Keep talking to him and reinforcing the idea that these goals are yours and his and that they must be met. Make certain that he knows that you really believe in the goals. A leader's confidence is very persuasive. At some point in time, he needs to come across the divide. If that does not happen, then you may need to move him out of the unit.

Sam: My boss gave me a new set of goals six months ago, and I do not agree with them. I do not know what to do about it.

The Doctor: Well, if you have never in those six months talked to your boss about these goals, you are in big trouble. Although I would have preferred that your boss get a clear acknowledgment that you accept the goals, it is nevertheless reasonable for your boss to conclude that your lack of feedback was an acceptance of the goals. It sounds like you did not take the goals seriously when they were assigned, and now that you realize that your boss is actually expecting you to make the goals, you have decided to object. Sorry, but if I were your boss, I would be pretty unhappy. Assuming that you are a leader and have other staff members you are responsible for, you have let them down by not dealing with this problem long ago. Your staff is going to get painted with the failure brush right along with you.

All of that said, I have two suggestions: 1) Talk to your boss and tell him that you made a mistake and should have discussed the goals much earlier. Explain your concerns, and then make it clear to your boss that you are going to make every effort to recover the rest of the year and would like his help in doing so. 2) Talk to your staff and work with them to achieve those goals.... you owe that to them, your boss and to yourself. Then...next year, speak up if you think that you have been assigned goals which cannot be met.

DAY 10

MIX IT UP

IN THE MODERN AGE of "politically correct" speech, several buzz words have gained prominence in our workplace dialogue, particularly the term "diversity". Diversity, as it pertains to the make-up of an organization, means having employees who bring different backgrounds, perspectives and talents to create a varied yet cohesive team. Unfortunately, being politically correct escalated to levels that bordered on the absurd, and many of the terms from that movement have been tainted by the extremism. Whereas "diversity" once had significant meaning, it has now become a hollow member of PC jargon. Leaders who are serious about success should put aside any PC-speak biases and embrace diversity as a means to complement their own talents and make up for their weaknesses.

Even the most renowned leaders have phenomenal talents in some areas and incredible weaknesses in others. It may not be easy for us as individuals to identify or admit our weaknesses, but they exist. Successful leaders make up for their shortcomings by filling the ranks with people who have the talents and abilities that they lack. This is where diversity plays a tangible role in the success of an organization as a whole. A group of individuals with similar origins, philosophies and talents will result in a homogenous and harmonious team but will fail to produce the award-winning, record-breaking achievements that make the difference between good and great.

The first step in building a team that will complement your abilities and goals is to honestly assess your personal strengths and weaknesses. Are you right- or left-brained? Do you have a million creative ideas yet struggle when it comes to discipline and organization? Or are you so practical and regimented that it is hard for you to let go and indulge in crazy ideas? Your talents and tendencies may not be that extreme, but if you are honest with yourself, you will be able to pinpoint the areas where you have a personal advantage and those where you have a disadvantage.

To accurately assess your strengths and weaknesses, you will need to get feedback from others. This requires putting your ego and sensitivity on a hiatus and reminding yourself that this endeavor is a means to enhance your success. Then ask your family, friends and colleagues what they think about your personal attributes and talents. The culmination of this review should be specific knowledge of the ways in which you excel and an understanding of the areas in which you need assistance.

The next step is to assess the ways in which your associates complement you, as well as their individual talents and advantages. Do they make up for your weaknesses? Do they replicate your thinking or do they offer different perspectives? Particularly in interview settings, we are drawn to the people we easily identify with because they have similar backgrounds and points of view. However, if we surround ourselves with people who are just like us, we lose the chance to improve on our individual abilities through the help of others. Use diversity as a tool to overcome your personal limitations and leverage what others can do to complement our own talents.

Diversity can sometimes lead to personality conflicts and differences of opinion that impede teamwork. The differences can be overcome, and diverse people can work harmoniously together, but it is up to the leader to make certain that all of the associates come together and support each other in reaching the team's goal. If you've ever watched the television show "The Apprentice", you have seen the impact that the leader has on a diverse team. The people vying to be the next apprentice for Donald Trump are a diverse group, from a wide variety of backgrounds and professions and they hardly know each other. The team leaders rotate on a project by project basis, and under one leader's direction a team may work well together and "win". Under another leader's direction, that team may fight, fail to be supportive of each other and ultimately "lose" the challenge. While reality television doesn't always seem like "real life", it is true that the same team of people will behave differently based on the leader's ability to unite the team.

When you solicit (and listen to) opinions other than your own and show respect and appreciation for your associates' various talents, you will set the right tone as the leader. Some leaders find that teamwork training or company retreats help their associates get past the barriers that their differences may create. The best way to avoid those barriers and problems is to demonstrate though your example that all employees are treated with equal and unconditional respect.

Having a diverse team of associates will help you to maximize each individual's strengths, as well as improve results with your clients and customers. It is likely that your customers have diverse backgrounds, so the diversity of your team will make you better equipped to serve them. If success is your goal, embrace diversity.

SECTION II: Mini Case — Taking Sides

Dana had been the Senior Account Manager at the East Coast headquarters of national advertising agency for the last four years. Recently, the West Coast office had been losing clients and their revenues were significantly less than in recent years. As a result, the West Coast President was fired and Dana was promoted to replace him. Although she was a little uneasy about adjusting to a new home and lifestyle in Los Angeles, Dana was thrilled with her promotion and career advancement. Having been very successful as a team leader in the past, as well as being very popular with the clients, she felt certain that she could make the West Coast office successful.

At her first creative meeting with the office staff, she told the Senior Account Manager, Jerrod, to lead the meeting as usual and that she would simply observe. Jerrod briefly described a new clients' latest product and the guidelines for an ad campaign that they were to create. He then asked everyone in the room to quickly come up with a couple slogan ideas, and then he called on everyone in turn to share their thoughts. He picked two slogans that he liked the most, and then asked everyone in the room to brainstorm for creative ideas to go with the slogans in a print ad. Up to this point Dana had thought that the meeting was going well and that Jerrod was a good leader.

As the brainstorming proceeded, Dana observed the group polarize into two teams. The teams clearly supported a particular slogan, and possibly its creator, and they only offered ideas for their favorite. When ideas were suggested for the slogan they didn't favor, they scoffed and often made critical and rude comments. Dana couldn't believe what she was seeing and hearing. In her experience leading the team on the East Coast, they had been a diverse group, which is typical for a profession that demands creativity, but they had gotten along together. There had been some good-natured teasing at times, but certainly nothing that approached the hostility she was witnessing in this group. She was further stunned by the fact that Jerrod carried on as if this were typical and acceptable behavior.

Following the meeting, Dana went to her office to think over the situation. She believed that the polarization and lack of respect among the team members were the reason that the office has not been performing well. Furthermore, their behavior indicated that only half of the team would work hard on this new campaign based on whether their favored idea was chosen. She questioned whether Jerrod was an effective leader because he had failed to unite his team. If she simply replaced him would the team work together, or were their personality conflicts insurmountable? She knew that she had to do something or the office would continue to fail and she would lose her job.

What should Dana do?

Dana could fire Jerrod and hope that the team dynamic improves under new leadership. But she is correct in questioning whether this will solve the problem, or whether certain members of the team will continue to create conflict and opposition. If she fires Jerrod and ultimately learns that the team can't work together, it may be too late to save her job. She could also fire the entire group, but building a great team takes time and it is likely that at least a handful of her associates are very talented and productive. How can she determine who to keep and who to let go?

She should start by having a long talk with Jerrod about her observations from the meeting. His tacit acceptance of the hostility cannot continue if the situation is to be improved, but

Dana may not have to replace him. Perhaps the former President accepted this behavior, or even set the tone for it himself. If that is the case, Jerrod may be able to improve as a leader and together they can change the culture to one of respect. Dana needs to make it clear to him that respect and cooperation are the only behaviors he should accept from his team. Jerrod may also be able to shed light on whether there are certain individuals who instigate the conflicts or refuse to support others' ideas. Those individuals should be coached to change, and if that doesn't work they should be replaced. Perhaps the entire group would benefit from coaching and teamwork training to foster trust and respect. Only when the individuals buy-in to their responsibility for supporting the team will they be able to achieve success.

SECTION III — The Doctor's Rx

We all have a "comfort zone" of people and activities that put us at ease. Although it may be difficult and feel awkward, it is important to put yourself outside of that zone on a routine basis. Exposure to ideas, perspectives, knowledge and cultures that are new or foreign to you will be personally enlightening and enriching. Those who stay glued to the safety of what is familiar miss out on the incredible experiences and opportunities that arise from trying something new. To enhance your personal and professional development, resolve to do a few of the following:

- Attend networking events. Meeting new people is ideal for cultivating business and personal relationships.
- Choose a personal hobby and join a club or group that is based on that hobby. If you enjoy playing a sport, join a local team. If you like to cook, join a gourmet club. Whatever group you choose, the other members will

share a common interest but are likely to have diverse backgrounds.

- Volunteer at a local charity that supports something for which you feel passionately. There is nothing more rewarding than helping.
- Look in the newspaper for local events such as seminars or speeches that cover topics of interest to you. Instead of clipping the ad and forgetting about it, sign up and go.
- Make an effort to change your routine and expand your horizons. If you like to read fiction, commit to alternating with nonfiction, biographies and other books from which you can learn something new.
- Follow up with people you meet and make a date for coffee or lunch to get to know them better.
- Make a list of all of the cultural "things" that you say you want to do but never make time for such as going to a local museum, the zoo, a pro sporting event or taking a day trip to a nearby town. Set a recurring date in your calendar, even if it is just once a month, to do one of the things on that list.

SECTION IV — Ask the Doctor

Lisa: My boss wants me to attend Chamber and other networking events in hopes that it will help build our business. The problem is that I don't enjoy these events and rarely meet someone who is a real prospect for our services. The scenario is always the same: I'm standing around alone because I don't know anyone and then I'm accosted by the "business-card vultures", or I make small talk with the few people I know from previous events. I leave with a bunch of business cards but no leads. Maybe if I were more aggressive it would produce better results, but the vulture approach doesn't fit my personality.

The Doctor: You must understand that networking is "work". If it were only fun and socializing, I'm sure you would choose to meet with your friends rather than a room full of strangers. When you learn how to network effectively, it will be less painful but it will not be easy. Being effective does not mean becoming a "vulture" because, as you know from experience, that technique is a complete turn-off. I recommend that you follow my "Four Steps for Successful Networking" so that you approach these events with a strategic plan.

First, assess the types of individuals and businesses that would be your top leads or referrals, and target two or three groups (local Chambers are usually excellent choices) where those people are likely to be members. Attend as many of their events as possible, and over time you will get to know more people and feel more comfortable.

Second, come up with a short sound bite that is a memorable and unique way of explaining what you do. In a crowd of people who are all there to make contacts and build their customer base, you need to stand out. A consultant I know says "I teach salespeople how to stop selling." That takes most people by surprise, and she follows up with a quick explanation that her training is based on the philosophy that "if you're telling, you're not selling." Her philosophy leads to the third strategy: ask questions.

When you meet someone, ask 1. what they do 2. how long they've been doing it 3. what they like about it and 4. what would be a good referral for them. Then move on and meet someone new. If a person wants to talk at length and is a legitimate lead, suggest getting together over lunch so that the two of you will have a better chance to discuss how you might help each other. If you're cornered and need an escape, simply introduce the person you're stuck with to someone near you, even if you don't know that person.

Fourth, whenever possible, help the people you meet by introducing them to their target referrals. If someone wants to meet lawyers and you know one in the room, make the introduction. When you help others, they will be more inclined to help you. The corollary to this is identifying your own targets and asking for introductions.

Networking is essential in all aspects of our lives, from building business referrals to making friends. People who are good at networking are usually the ones who listen more than they talk. Who doesn't like to talk about themselves and the things that are important to them? Your strategy should be to ask questions and listen, which will help you determine how their interests or needs intersect with your own.

11

PEAK PERFORMANCE

ALL LEADERS WANT THEIR teams to aim for, and achieve, Peak Performance. In my book, <u>You're In Charge… What Now</u>, I use that term to describe the leader's "end game." Most athletes understand peak performance, and they are constantly training their physical and mental processes to achieve it. In the world of athletics, achieving beyond that which seems physically possible is the standard for teams and individual athletes who aim for excellence. In this context, peak performance means pushing the body of the athlete to perform at levels that exceed that of the competitor, as well as the athletes' personal expectations.

Superior athletes like those winning the Ironman, or the "greats" such as Lance Armstrong and Tiger Woods, all share a set of key characteristics:

1. They have physically superior stamina, strength and athletic ability

2. They have the discipline to practice their sport on a rigorous and consistent basis to develop the skills necessary to achieve excellence

3. They have an emotional and intellectual commitment to achieving success

4. They have the capacity to manage the stress of competition so that it does not adversely affect their ability to perform.

Success in achieving peak performance requires all of these attributes to be executed during competition; after which, rest, recovery and renewal are essential to reinvigorate the athlete and the team.

Sports analogies have been used for years to compare the leadership skills applied in athletics to those required in the business world. Though not perfect, these analogies can be helpful in taking the lessons learned from sports competition and applying them to the achievement of organizational success and peak performance.

In the working world, peak performance means that the organization and its staff is achieving excellence. Most leaders attempt to maximize the quality of the team's performance within the constraints of organization's material means and personnel. Aiming for excellence has a competitive foundation, but when a leader strives for peak performance it is the result of that leader's desire to achieve more than the expectations of the organization.

The quest for peak performance in athletics has some striking parallels and critical differences to that quest in the working world. The first athletic criteria of physical stamina, strength and athletic ability, plays a far less significant role in business. Strength and athletic ability are trivial; however, stamina, or the ability to sustain energetic effort, does play an important role and may be a significant factor for success. The associates in an organization must have the ability to maintain a consistent, focused effort in order to achieve peak performance.

The second element of sustained disciplined and practice plays a huge part in an organization's ability to achieve peak performance. Superior organizations commit significant amounts of time, energy and money to develop the knowledge and skills necessary to execute effectively. Peak performance hinges on the ability of the associates, and in turn the organization, to learn and exercise the skills that will accomplish the mission of the organization. It is essential that an organization is committed to achieving sustained performance through training and development. Exercising discipline, and maintaining a commitment to the system's procedures and processes, separates the occasional success from the sustained peak performance.

The third criterion for athletes is the will, commitment and great desire to achieve success. This is every bit as critical in business as it is in athletics. Organizational leadership drives peak performance by building a culture of commitment to success. In a peak performing organization, mediocrity is not an acceptable objective. Superior performance and just rewards spark the associates' desire to contribute to the peak performance of the organization. The leader's role in building a culture of commitment to success is the most significant contribution that the leader can make in achieving peak performance. Raw ability, talent and stamina will only translate to successful achievement when the culture in the organization embraces peak performance as the only acceptable goal.

Peak performance requires the ability to manage stress. An athlete must be "on" during competitions but is able to rejuvenate between those events. In the business world, there is really no pause or down time in striving for peak performance. In many ways each day, indeed every minute of every day, is a competitive moment. This continuous battle against the competition leaves very little rejuvenation time for the individuals or the organization. Yet, like the individual athlete or sports team, the organization must provide the opportunity for renewal. This renewal can be in a variety of ways: vacations for the associates; company-sponsored events away from the workplace; sabbaticals; retreats; training sessions or simply good humor. The leader must recognize that consistent and sustained peak performance is not possible without time for refreshment, reflection and renewal. Just as an athlete or a sports team must be given an opportunity to recuperate its energy and vitality, so must the organization be given an opportunity to "re-charge its batteries".

SECTION II: Mini Case — Sam Pushes For Excellence

Sam is the manager of the accounts receivable department at a Fortune 500 company. For many years, his department has achieved reasonable success but it has never been recognized as outstanding. Sam is new at this job and is highly motivated to translate his own personal excellence in athletics into leadership that will help his organization produce superior results.

Sam played basketball in high school and in college where he was part of a conference winning team. He was always recognized as an individual with average skill but substantially above average commitment, passion and drive to win. That same drive and passion to achieve has helped him in his career. He worked long hours, stayed focused on results and impressed his boss with his knowledge, skills and discipline. After two years with this company, he was promoted to manager. He bypassed many of his peers who had been there longer, and they are less than pleased with his quick rise to management status. Few of them have any real prospect of moving up or out even thought they are talented accountants with good training and experience. The difference is that they did not demonstrate any real commitment to the company or to their department.

After two months as head of the department, Sam has made every effort to raise the bar on his team's expectations and achievement. The results have been consistently mediocre. The others have not bought into Sam's vision of achieving superior peak performance. Sam frequently finds himself compensating for their mediocrity by working well into the night. He talked to his boss about the problem; and although sympathetic, his boss offered few suggestions. Sam is highly competitive and knows that if he does not achieve superior results in his department it will negatively impact his career. He will be at risk of being in the same stagnant position as the rest of the associates in his department.

The Doctor: What options does Sam have in turning around the department performance and creating an organization that truly does strive for peak performance?

Sam's problem is not unique. Most new managers who have moved up the ranks from individual performer to supervisor have a similar difficulty. As an individual performer, success rests on our own shoulders; our personal energy and commitment coupled with core knowledge and skill can propel us to achieve recognition and promotion. The question to ask Sam is "You're in Charge... What Now?" The "what now" is for Sam to understand that leading an organization requires more than setting a good example. In business, enthusiasm, commitment and energy may play a role in encouraging performance but it differs from athletics in that it is not going to motivate the team to go above and beyond their previous performance levels.

Sam needs to learn all of the messages in the leader's mnemonic before he can become an effective peak performance leader. His biggest problem may be that he is not yet able to "love" his associates. Until he convinces them that he truly cares about them as human beings he cannot persuade them to care about his organizational goals. Furthermore, Sam should not continue to make up for their inadequacies by working longer hours himself. He must establish expectations, hold his staff accountable to those expectations and eventually reward those who perform. Sam also needs to consider how much he is asking of them in light of their own abilities and commitments. He may need to get a few "new associates on the bus." Sam cannot be the only individual performer striving for peak performance. The fallacy in typical leadership advice is that one can "motivate" anybody. At the end of the day, if an individual does not have the inherent desire to achieve, no amount of motivational behavior on the leader's part will elicit peak performance from that associate.

SECTION III — The Doctor's Rx

For those of you who have experienced winning in athletics or other competitions, the sports analogy can be powerful. Enthusiasm, commitment, discipline, stamina, finely developed skills and the desire to win all have a place both in sports and in the world of work. In sports, winning probably required physical and athletic prowess, coordination and strength. Whether as an individual performer such as in golf, or a as part of a team performance such as in basketball, the end result was the use of those physical skills to achieve success.

In the world of work, leading people effectively requires many of the same skills it took to be an effective leader in athletics, but it also requires technical knowledge, process orientation, business acumen, organizational structure and design and the ability to understand the profit motive and financial controls. Take the learning from the world of athletic competition and temper it with the recognition that the vast majority of us in the working world are what Peter Drucker called "knowledge workers". Consequently, the key skill we will deploy is that of intellectual or mental prowess, not physical prowess. There is indeed a difference between shooting a basket and designing a ship.

SECTION IV — Ask the Doctor

David: I've been in charge of a three person sales force for the past year, and we have missed virtually all of our sales goals. I am, or at least was, a great salesman. I became the sales manager because I far exceeded every sales goal put in front of me, and my boss was convinced that I could get team to do the same thing. Under my leadership, I think that the individual salespeople have actually fallen in their performance level and are selling less than before I took over. I know that is what my boss believes, and I suspect that I'm in trouble as a result. I expect that he will put me back as a salesman and bring in somebody else to manage the sales force. I guess secretly I would prefer that, but I've never failed in anything that I've done in the world of work so failing at this is really hard for me to swallow. What can I do?

The Doctor: David, you are not the first great salesman to be promoted to sales manager and then to fail in that role and I doubt that you will be the last. I think you know what you can do, because you have already suggested it at the end of your letter. You know you really do not like being in charge, and as you said "I guess secretly I would prefer that." It seems to me that tells it all, and you've given yourself the best advice available. The problem is not what you should do; the problem is how to reconcile the decision to step down from being manager with your own ego thinking that it is a failure.

There is very little that I can do to help you with that except to say that you may just not be ready to be in charge, not that you cannot be effective at that someday. It is clear that you enjoy and excel at selling and are frustrated by being in charge. I suggest you simply accept that reality and go back to being the best salesman you know how to be. Take some time, reorient yourself to your success as a salesman and then consider taking some training in the skills that are required to be an effective leader. I recommend that you continue to read my books and reflect on what it takes to be a good leader. The day may come when it will once again be time for you to become a manager. With a little time, and learning, plus a lot more enthusiasm for being "in charge," you could become an excellent leader.

IS YOUR BUS FULL OF STARS?

JIM COLLINS IN HIS BOOK, Good to Great, talks a great deal about a metaphor of "the bus." He says that if you want to drive your team and organization to success, you have to fill each seat with only the best people and consequently vacate the seats occupied by the weakest. The essence of his message is one that I also stressed in my book, You're In Charge…What Now?, and it reflects my conviction that you cannot build an organization that achieves excellence if you have the wrong people on your staff. In fact, I believe that you cannot build a superior organization unless you consistently and effectively recruit and retain the "stars."

Many of you might be thinking "Great idea, but the world is not made of stars, it is made up of far more average performers. I cannot find enough stars, and besides, their expectations are beyond my ability to meet." Such a mindset will only ensure that neither you, nor your organization, will achieve great success.

One of the chapters in my book is entitled, "An Organization Elicits the Behavior it Rewards." I would counter your argument with a new chapter, "An Organization Achieves the Performance for Which It Staffs."

If you are willing to recruit, hire and retain mediocre talent, you will get mediocre results. I realize that there have been some sports teams that have achieved greatness with what were defined as "journeyman players," but frankly, I think they are all myths. The Green Bay Packers team under Coach Lombardi have been held out as such a team, but when we look at the resulting performances of those previously labeled "journeymen" we find that they may have had the appearance of such, but they were stars who had not achieved their potential. This was the secret weapon of Coach Lombardi, and it must be the secret of every leader, no matter what type of organization.

Your goal should be to find those people who have the knowledge, skills, attitudes and raw talent that will make them stars in your organization. This may require a special talent that you as an individual have not yet mastered, but it is a skill that you must either develop or borrow from someone who will assist you in recruiting. Some stars are obvious, and you should recognize and pursue them immediately. Decide who you want, then find a way to hire them. Success at hiring is not just about money, it is about having a job that "turns them on" and a workplace environment, including your leadership, which causes an associate to say, "I want to work for that organization and that leader."

Your determination to enthusiastically convince and sell the prospective employee is essential. Great prospects need to know that you really want them to be a part of the team and that you are committed to helping them achieve their goals. I have a very high conversion rate on my employment offers because I make the job seem like the only one that could fulfill the applicants' goals, and furthermore that I would do everything in my power to help them achieve those goals. You can inspire the same feelings among your prospects, but you must also believe in the truth of your promises and your ability to bring them to fruition.

In addition to recognizing the obvious stars, you need to look for the "hidden stars" that possess raw, unpolished talent. Not every potential star looks like one, but potential stars have some key characteristics in common:

1. They are bright and curious,
2. They have not just a desire, but a need, to succeed and more importantly, to achieve,
3. They have a strong ethical foundation,
4. They are not afraid of hard work and
5. They enjoy life and what they do.

When I find a candidate with these characteristics (irrespective of what their resume says), I am likely to decide that they have the potential behavioral features I want on my team. It is a plus if they happen to have technical skills already, but with those inherent qualities alone will probably be sufficient for me to bet in them as potential stars. You need to learn how to find these "uncut diamonds" because they are the real finds. These are people who are stars already, but they do not know it, and the world has yet to see the results of their abilities and qualities.

Hiring stars is the first critical step, but you cannot stop there. You must commit to making certain that each "star" is given the best you have to offer. They must be given great orientations, productive and challenging assignments and they must be given focused coaching. If all you do is hire them, assign them a job and then leave them to achieve on their own, you may take a potential star and turn them into an average performer. If you have adopted my assertion that you must love your associates, then you must not fail to provide them with leadership and challenge. Focus on the stars, keep them challenged and help them create a new future for themselves and for your organization.

SECTION II: Mini Case — The Painful Job Search

Nathalie will graduate from her local state university next month and has been interviewing for her first "real job" for the past five months. The process has been long and painful. As a communications major at a highly-regarded university, Nathalie has been a super-achiever who earned outstanding grades, participated in many school activities, played sports, held leadership positions in two student organizations, and worked at night to finance her education. While she has been invited to interview with several companies, she has been frustrated by the fact that most are looking for technical backgrounds such as engineering, accounting, statistics or even marketing. The process has been discouraging, and her failure to get a meaningful job offer has made her very concerned about how she will pay her student loans once she is out of school.

Her discouragement and worry have escalated with the passing of the days and months, and have caused Nathalie to set her sights lower and lower. Consequently, she has had several interviews recently for jobs that she would not have considered taking just a few short months ago. Her last interview was for a job that she knows she could have gotten right out of high school.

In contrast to Nathalie, her friend June is an accounting major who has had five job offers in the last three weeks. June is only a mediocre student, but the offers keep coming. Nathalie knows that she would never enjoy being an accountant, but has recently thought she should have studied something more practical so that she could be in June's enviable position. Nathalie has another job interview tomorrow with a high-tech firm looking for a sales representative, and is worried that she will be rejected once again because she has no sales or marketing experience.

Issue: What is the likely outcome of Nathalie's dilemma? Can she do anything to change her job prospects? As an interviewer, what would be your view of Nathalie as a potential employee?

There is a strong possibility that Nathalie needs help with her interview skills. Her frustration and failure to get job offers might have caused her to lose self-confidence or become defensive during interviews. Nathalie should ask someone with experience to critique her through a role-play interview and then evaluate whether she is part of the problem.

In addition to the interview itself, Nathalie has two more hurdles to overcome. The first is that she really did not pick a field that sells well in an era where companies are looking for specific skills. The second is that it sounds as though she has had the misfortune of interviewing with people who simply could not look past her resume. If she is as talented and focused as she appears, then there are many companies out there who have lost the chance to hire a "hidden star." Hopefully a bright, creative interviewer will look past the fact that she lacks experience or specific skills; but that in her academic career she has demonstrated great qualities and strengths that can be developed into stardom in her professional career.

SECTION III — The Doctor's Rx

Interviewing candidates is almost an "art form." Most of us who do interviews do them only when we need a new staff member. Typically we spend far too little time in preparation, and probably far too little time in the interview itself. When you are looking for a new associate, you might be short on time for anything but the most critical activities that are required to "get the work out." If that is your plight, then follow these strategies for successful interviewing:

a. Allow at least an hour to talk to the candidate. Twenty minute interviews are just too short. By the time you get comfortable with the process, the interview is over.

b. Conduct the interview in a place that is comfortable for both you and the applicant. If you are uncomfortable, you will try to rush the interview. If the applicants are uncomfortable, they will be stressed and will not be at their best.

c. Ask questions that cannot be answered with a yes or no. Make certain that the questions require the applicant to think and communicate.

d. Be careful that you do not let the resume dominate your conversation. You will gain better insight if you listen to what the candidates want to talk about, or what they think you want to talk about. Discussion should be based on the things that will most influence your decision as t whether the candidate has what it takes to work for your organization.

e. Try to assess how smart, committed to hard work and skilled the person is. These traits cannot be determined by discussing what school they attended. If you ask about school, then focus on the education --what they actually learned, not what grades they received.

SECTION IV — Ask the Doctor

Ted: I am the supervisor of a five person sales force and I have just lost three of my staff members. I am almost in a panic, because all three will be leaving in two weeks, and I have no clue how I am going to find replacements, especially in that timeframe. What should I do?

The Doctor: Losing 60% of my staff all at once would probably put me in a panic as well. You do have a challenge, but before we address how to find replacements, you need to ask yourself why the three people are leaving at the same time. Perhaps it is a coincidence, but it could be much more serious than that. You should also consider whether their departure might actually be a good thing. If you are losing your three worst performers, it is a great deal better than losing your three best.

The first step in moving forward is to talk with those who are leaving and try to find out the reason. If they will not give you a clear answer, then seek additional assistance. If you work for a large enough organization, you may have a HR department that will do exit interviews for you. Former employees are often more willing to talk to a third party… it is worth a try. You should anticipate the fact that you will not like their reasons for leaving, and be prepared to take a hard look at weaknesses in yourself or the organization.

When you know what caused their departure, then you can start to do something about it. If they are leaving because of something you or the organization is doing wrong, then you need to focus your energy on fixing that problem…ASAP! It makes no sense to hire more people if you are going to have a mass exodus again in a few months. If the situation really is just a coincidence, or if your staff has been lured away by a competing organization, or if they decided to leave for three totally different reasons beyond your control, you still need to focus on those root causes.

Let's assume that the three say they left because they simply had a better offer. This is not a very useful answer and is often a mask to cover over the real reason. I would suggest that, aside from a true coincidence, you have a leadership problem that can either be attributed to you or to your company. Regardless of who or what is to blame, the problem will cause frequent employee turnover in the future as well.

In the event that these were actually your three worst associates, then despite the bad-timing of their departure, it is possibly the best thing that could have happened to you. It probably means that they got the message you had been sending about their performance. You should have been looking for replacements much sooner, but now is a great time to make certain that you get the right people on "the bus."

DAY 13

FINDING THE RIGHT FIT

ASK THE LEADERS OF A peak performing business what the secret is to their success and you will usually hear that it is the people who work for them. Having great employees is every leader's goal; however, determining who will be a great fit in your organization requires discipline and commitment. If you don't approach the hiring process as one of your most important activities as a leader, you are most likely not going to have a team of superstars working for you. If you invest your attention and energy toward hiring a potential star, you are much more likely to have the desired result.

The process starts with writing a detailed job description. The first aspect should define the expectations. What outcomes should the work produce? The second aspect is to define the variety of the tasks and assignments that will be required to achieve the expected outcomes. What actions does this job entail on a daily basis? The third aspect is to define the core requirements to be able to do the job. Is there a level of education, technical skills or other criteria that are needed?

When the job description is complete, make a list of the key characteristics that a successful candidate would possess. Some of the characteristics should be based on ability and others on personality or attitude. The goal in this phase is to consider your management style, the culture of the workplace and other particular aspects of the job that would make a person either mesh or clash with the organization. A good way to make this determination is to assess what made others succeed or fail in this position. When you know what you are looking for, write an ad that includes the details of the job description and desired characteristics. You want the ad to attract great candidates, so it is wise to include some information about the company and why it's such a great place to work.

In the resume filtering and interviewing phase, keep your expectations high. If you settle for a candidate who only partially satisfies your requirements, that person is not going to be a star performer. How do you determine from a resume and interview who will be a star? A resume is a wealth of information, but the interview will be your key to discovery. Ask questions about their past employment that will give you insight into their achievements. Prior behavior is a great predictor of future behavior. Look for people who have demonstrated success for their previous employers. Spend time probing into the candidate's history of accomplishments, learning and growth potential. When you have given the hiring process a concentrated effort, you will be faced with tough decisions but will be likely to find the right fit: a candidate who matches your expectations of knowledge, skills and attitudes.

SECTION II: Mini Case — The Assistant Who Won't Assist

Jennifer is the Senior Vice President of Marketing in a large company that develops and sells software for medical systems in hospitals and doctors' offices. Her new assistant, Steve, has been working under her supervision for the last six weeks and she is delighted with his progress. Unlike the previous assistant who lacked competence in simple administrative work and had to be let go, Steve has caught on fairly quickly. Now that he has learned the various systems for managing her calendar, contacts database and billing, Jennifer is ready to give him some assignments to assist her in marketing the company's software.

She sets a meeting with Steve to review the action plan that she gave him when he started the job. Having reviewed the plan herself, she sees that he has accomplished the initial tasks and with her guidance will now be able to start with the marketing related tasks. When the meeting starts, Jennifer tells Steve how pleased she is with his performance thus far, and that she feels he is ready to take on some of the additional responsibilities outlined in the job description.

"Steve, here is a list of hospitals and doctors' offices in the next county that we have not yet approached to sell our software," Jennifer said. "I would like you to call each of them, ask for the name of the person who manages the office or technical systems, and then send a pitch letter to that person. I'll provide you with a sample letter that I have used. When the letters have gone out, we'll wait a couple days and then make follow up calls to them."

Jennifer was surprised that Steve didn't react to the new assignment with any questions. He simply took the list and left. A few days later she followed up with him and inquired about the status of the letters. Steve looked at her with a somewhat hostile expression on his face and said "I don't make cold calls and this was not part of my job description." Jennifer was stunned. She was upset that he had been silent on the matter for the last days and had simply ignored the assignment. She also knew that assisting with marketing was specifically outlined in the job description as well as the action plan that he was given on the first day of employment. Rather than give a knee-jerk reaction, Jennifer said she would take some time to consider the situation.

The Doctor: What should Jennifer do?

It appears that Jennifer has been a good supervisor in regards to providing a full and detailed job description, as well as a list of short and long term assignments. She is now faced with the question of whether to fire another assistant, despite the fact that he has been satisfactory in his performance up to this point. The prospect of starting over, looking for a new candidate and ultimately training a new hire is not a pleasant one. On the other hand, retaining an employee who refuses to even attempt an assignment that is part of his job description indicates that he is the wrong person for the job. It also indicates a lack of ambition and lack of commitment to furthering the goals of the organization.

Jennifer should have a conversation with him and say that she has been pleased with his previous performance but that assisting her in marketing is not an optional part of the job, it is required. She can then show him the job description as a reminder and ask him if he is still uncomfortable with the assignment. It is not likely that he will heartily and convincingly persuade her that he wants the assignment. In that case, she should tell him that he is not the right fit for the job and let him go.

SECTION III — The Doctor's Rx

All of us have been in the interviewee seat, but many people who are promoted to a leadership role have never been the interviewer. Following are some guidelines for conducting a successful interview:

Define the Position

- Describe the duties, technical knowledge and skills required
- Identify the factors that will lead to success in this job
- Establish the expectations of performance and accomplishment ask and then listen
- Determine a set of questions in advance that will help evaluate whether the person fits the requirements
- Ask behavior based questions for candidates to share specific experiences that demonstrate their abilities or achievements
- Probe into the details with follow up questions to their answers
- Ask attitude related questions to determine whether the personality is a fit with the office culture
- Listen intently and let them do the talking
- Whenever possible, have more than one person interview the candidates

SECTION IV — Ask the Doctor

Dan: I was recently promoted to Vice President of Sales for a company that sells telecommunication systems. My promotion stemmed from the fact that I was the top performing salesman in the company last year, and the previous VP retired. My company is growing, and now we need to increase our sales force. The first two people I hired were not successful in making sales and I had to let them go. I think I'm pretty good at evaluating candidates, but I must be missing something. Can you give me some tips on how to identify someone who will be good in sales?

The Doctor: There is no magic formula for identifying a good salesperson. Individuals who work in sales have to possess the unique personality blend of being both gregarious and independent. They have to be socially outgoing because they need to interact with all types of people. They also have to be comfortable on their own because they will typically be traveling alone to make sales calls. You can easily assess candidates' social skills by how they present themselves and communicate during the interview. To determine their independence, simply ask them if they need to be with people or if they work happily alone. To get a feel for their drive and ability to achieve, ask about their previous experiences, greatest accomplishments and future goals. Finally, ask them to sell you on why they should be selected for the job. If they can't sell themselves they can't sell.

You said that you were the top seller in your company, so ask yourself what qualities and skills have made you so successful. Ask your boss and, perhaps your clients, to help define what makes you good at selling telecommunication systems. Make a list of those qualities and skills, and then evaluate each candidate based on that list. Is it your winning personality, your technical knowledge of the product, your years of experience? The factors that have lead to your success should be indicators of what you are looking for in a candidate.

14

FALLING SHORT
OF EXPECTATIONS

AT TIMES IN MY CAREER as a leader, my organization, or at least one part of it, has fallen short of expectations. Leaders may work hard to make certain that everybody knows and understands the organization's expectations, and yet the associates still fall short on delivering. I consciously call this "falling short" rather than "failing" not because I am afraid to call a missed expectation a failure when I see it, but because falling short is not always failure.

Your staff may do a phenomenal job, but fail to meet expectations because they were too high to begin with. Their shortfall could also be a failure on their part to achieve; or it could be a failure on your part to effectively set the expectations, and ensure achievement. It is the staff's responsibility to work diligently to achieve the expectations, but is also the duty of the leader to support achievement. As leaders, we must recognize our role and responsibility in supporting our associates' achievement and success.

Development is a key responsibility of leaders, and it involves more than merely training the staff. It also goes beyond simply giving feedback on results and having "after the fact" discussions. Development requires coaching the staff to success. It is through coaching, or the lack thereof, that we can often find the explanation for our associates' failure.

The coach of the college football team does not just review the game films and give the team feedback after their performance. If Joe, the star guard, misses a tackle, the coaches will quickly point out the blunder, but the extra accountability forced on that ballplayer is not where it stops. During the next week, the coaches will spend time with the entire team, and will focus on refining the skills of each player through practice, practice, practice. Those skills are essential and the coaches will work to assure themselves that they have "helped" each player and each team component to fix the deficiencies.

Coaching means being part teacher, part task master, part shoulder, and part parent. At the end of the day, each team member will have spent enough time in practice with the coaches that they will be tired of the workout. But they will have learned, though repetition, all of the plays. The coaches and players alike will be able to perform these tasks "in their sleep."

Coaching a football team does require a great deal of attention to skill in physical performance, but there is very little fundamental difference between this skill training and that of any other work-related skills. We must perform a variety of tasks in the work place, and our ability to be successful in those activities is tied directly to our skills in execution. We may not need to train our bodies to perform, but we must train our minds, and even our emotions, to achieve the results of the job. Every associate working for the leader must be able to "perform" and that performance is almost always related to a combination of skills and intellectual capacity. The most brilliant law school graduate still needs to learn how to apply legal principles to a "real world" law practice.

A leader's coaching skills are the single most important development tool available to encourage and facilitate an associate's achievement. Coaching can be a challenge because it requires dedicating a great deal of time and patience to help an associate who is new, naïve or struggling to find the proper skills required to achieve excellence. Furthermore, effective coaching is not possible if the coach is not personally competent in the associate's task or functional activity. The coach needs to have a practical, not just intellectual, understanding of the being supervised. The old saying, experience is the best teacher, truly applies to coaches.

I was recently working with the CEO of a company who was having a problem with his marketing and sales organization. He had spent a great deal of time and money developing solid market segmentation and sales messaging research on the key drivers for creating and effectively selling into his sales funnel. The research was conclusive and proved to be very accurate in predicting success.

During his last Sales Review meeting it became clear that the sales team has not been using the new disciplines that had been provided for them to maximize their effectiveness in the sales process. He was very troubled because he had spent many hours working with the sales force and the Sales Manager. Despite his thorough explanation of the data, the conclusions and how they should apply this to their sales process, the team had not implemented it. We talked for a quite some time and it became clear that the Sales Manager needed to do a great deal more coaching of the sales force members, and that seems to be exactly where the process had broken down. The Sales Manager was not getting the message across to the staff. As we discussed the problem, I asked if the Sales Manager had ever personally used the process steps to make a sale. He could not recall any instance when he had seen that occur. Our conclusion was that he needed to completely retrain his Sales Manager, because until he demonstrated competence in the process, it was impossible for him to coach his sales associates.

SECTION II: Mini Case — The Coach that Never Was

Jane has been the Vice President of Research Development for a large manufacturing company for over three years. In that time she and her staff have not pulled together adequately for one of the research projects to result in the creation of a major new product. This was severely disappointing to Jane because she had started the job with great hopes for success. While working as a senior researcher for her previous employer, she had been to a seminar on a new systems approach to product development. She had studied this systems methodology until she was an expert, and then applied it herself in the development of a new, breakthrough product for the company. Indeed, it was that product that had resulted in her new job and career advancement to VP of R&D at her current company.

Because of her disappointment during her first 19 months, Jane had completely re-staffed her organization with some of the best talent in her field. She fully expected that this highly talented staff would come together to develop a successful new product. Much to her chagrin, the staff has now been in place for almost ten months, and the team has still not been able to implement a process that would effectively create a breakthrough product.

So, what is wrong? – Jane seems to have the opposite problem from that of the Sales Manager in the previous case. The Sales Manager did not know and understand the process well enough to coach it. In this case, Jane knows the process extremely well, and has hands-on experience deploying the methodology. The problem must be that she has not taken the time to sell and coach her staff on the process. Jane may be leaving her staff to assimilate the process knowledge and deploy it on their own. My experience is that no matter how smart the staff, new processes require intense coaching for people to become accustomed to the techniques and the changes they require.

SECTION III — The Doctor's Rx

One question that often comes up about coaching is, "How do I know when I should coach?" My answer is to look for a few obvious, tell-tale signs:

1. Your staff is not following processes that you think you have made very clear
2. One or more associates are having quality problems in their output, while others with similar capabilities seem to be doing quite well.
3. You are surprised or even shocked to be receiving questions to which you think the answers should be obvious.
4. Somebody in the organization seems lost but cannot manage to ask you the right questions.
5. One or more of the associates are getting frustrated with their project or tasks, and their attitude is deteriorating.

In short, if your staff seems to be either lost or angry, they probably need help. Coaching is a leadership function that you should be doing every day, irrespective of your associates' performance and the state of the organization.

SECTION IV — Ask the Doctor

Stan: I have been "In Charge" of a small group of financial analysts for the last six months, and frankly, I am about to quit. I have been trying to coach them to achieve higher productivity levels and they are not even coming close to my expectations. It is almost as if they refuse to be coached.

The Doctor: You may be precisely right...they may actually be refusing to be coached. Unfortunately, there are some people who do refuse to be coached. It is possible that you have a serious problem with the staff's willingness to be lead by you or anybody else; alternatively, you may have a leadership problem yourself. If you are not connecting with the staff, they may have concluded that you are not a loving boss.

Another possible explanation is that you are wrong in trying to impose your own productivity strategy on the analysts. Financial analysts are intense, analytical people who focus on the content and the rigor of their work. They are not likely to be as receptive to productivity initiatives if they think that they will interfere with their intellectual thought process.

Perhaps you have some people who refuse to be lead because they have been around long enough to know that management is very happy with their work. If these analysts are actually highly-paid prima donnas, you may be "pushing a straw up a hill" in trying to get them to change their ways. I suggest that you back off the initiative and build a relationship with them first, then discuss productivity later.

DAY 15

THE FALLEN STAR

RECENTLY I WAS VISITING with a client who asked my advice in handling a situation with a young professional in his company who had recently missed some important project deadlines. As background, he told me that she is a graduate of one of the best universities in the nation and has a graduate degree in engineering from a major research institution in New England. Physics major with a Master's in electrical engineering is not a typical recruit for this firm, so from the beginning she was on a fast track within the organization. Her accomplishments over the three years that she has worked there have reinforced her incredible potential, and the management team views her as a "rising star". On every project assigned to her, she has proven both her intellect and her ability to be one of the most creative contributors in the organization.

My client told me he had given his "star" assignments that he thought would challenge her, and she has stepped up and delivered exceptional performance and clear evidence of growth. Her uncharacteristic failure to meet deadlines had first started about three months ago, around the same time that my client had reorganized the company's divisional structure. The CEO and I had been discussing for some time the need to flatten his organizational chart, and as a result the Division General Manager had actually taken a whole layer out of the organization. I was feeling really good about helping improve the responsiveness of the organization, as well as the money that would be saved by eliminating that unnecessary layer of management.

This change should have been positive for the "star engineer" because it gave her the chance to work directly for the Division General Manager as a staff engineer on special projects. This was perceived by the entire staff in the division as a phenomenal break for the young engineer, and it was clear to them that she was on her way up to bigger and better things in the company. Unfortunately, it hasn't worked out the way they expected. Almost from the inception of the reorganization, she started to behave in a way that was completely out of character with her previous performance. Practically overnight, she had gone from a rising star to a fallen star.

My client was upset and bewildered by her change in behavior, and asked me to help him find out what the problem was. I asked him what I thought was a rather obvious question: "What is her explanation for the change?" He said, "I don't know, I haven't talked to her about it." So I asked the next obvious question, "What does her boss tell you about her explanation?" He said, "Well, he has not talked to her about it either, so we are really still in the dark. That is why I asked you for your thoughts."

His answer left me quite disoriented, especially since I had been working with this client for over six months. I actually felt like a failure. It was inconceivable to me that this client, who was paying me to help him change the culture of his organization, could tell me that nobody had talked to the young woman about what was wrong. I truly thought that he had read enough of my book, and heard enough of my counsel to know that he had given me the "wrong answer." I was not disappointed in him nearly as much as I was in myself.

I explained to him how critical it is that somebody take the time to talk to the young "fallen star." One could come up with any number of plausible explanations for her change in behavior, which may or may not be work-related. Our conjecture about the source of her problem is irrelevant; the important point is what the associate could tell the organization.

Flying home on the plane that night, I spent an enormous amount of time brooding over my failure. As a "management guru" being paid a consulting fee to help a CEO become a better leader, focusing in large measure on helping that CEO develop his associates into superior performers, how had I failed to get the most basic of messages incorporated into his behavior? I was truly disappointed, and focused on searching for where I failed and what I needed to do. After a painful trip, I realized that I had fallen prey to my own version of the CEO's problem. I could not remember a single time when I explicitly said to my client or his General Manager, "You must remember to have a conversation with each of your key associates to let them know how well they are doing according to your expectations, and also to address any problems." Worse, I had never thought that they would need that advice. I had assumed they knew the right thing to do. Continuous communication with the staff, and having candid discussions with them about their work, was so obvious to me that I never mentioned it.

Assuming that what is obvious to us is equally obvious to others is a common mistake; and likewise, something that seems "simple" does not mean it is easy. How could my client not know that the best source of information regarding his associate's drop in performance would be a candid conversation with the associate herself? For whatever reason, he decided to ask me rather than the only person who could provide the answers. Direct and candid communication is not always the easiest thing to do, but more often than not, it will turn out to be the best. Once again, leading is pretty simple, but not always easy, and talking to a troubled subordinate is often the simplest course of action, but not the easiest.

SECTION II: Mini Case — Sonya is angry...Why?

Sonya was the lead analyst on the last four projects and she had "knocked the lights out" each time. Frank was so delighted with her performance that he had put in a request for her to receive a special, one-time bonus. He talked to his boss, who had readily endorsed the recommendation and submitted it to the Vice President of Information Technology. Three weeks had passed and Frank had heard nothing, so today he decided to ask his boss about the status of Sonya's bonus.

Frank went up to his boss's office on the third floor where he waited for him to get off the phone with the VP. When he went in, his boss told him, "I just talked to the VP, and he has turned down the bonus." Frank was shocked, "How could he do that? Sonya had done everything we asked her to do and much more. What was his reason?"

"I asked him that same question," his boss said, "and he said that they have run out of bonus money because the company's sales have been poor this month. He suggested that we come back for the bonus next month, because that it is normally a very strong month for sales and therefore it will be more likely that the company could afford the bonus."

"But I can't go back to the office without that bonus for Sonya," Frank said. His boss asked why and Frank said, "Because she knows that is why I am up here and she's expecting me to come back with a bonus check." Frank's boss was shocked and sympathetic, but told him that he had no choice but to go back and tell Sonya the truth.

Frank went back down to his office and told Sonya that the bonus has been turned down, and that maybe it would be possible the next month. Sonya got very upset and stormed out of his office telling him, "I am not certain what I am going to do, but it is clear to me that this company does not appreciate me, and does not think enough of me to recognize how much I contribute."

Issue: What happened? Why is Sonya upset, and what should Frank do now? How could this have been avoided?

The Doctor's Comments:

This is a great example of just what happens when a boss crosses over the line with candor. Frank has an open and candid relationship with Sonya; but in this case, Frank has disclosed more than he should have. In telling Sonya that he had recommended her for a bonus, he set them both up for disappointment and trouble.

As leaders, we must all make decisions about how much we share with our associates. Frank may have had the experience that his bonus recommendations were routinely approved, or he may have had no prior experience with requesting a bonus. There was no benefit in telling Sonya about the bonus prior to it being approved; on the contrary it was a risk to set high expectations that could potentially turn to disappointment should she not receive the bonus.

Frank probably wanted to show Sonya that he appreciated her work and was doing everything he could to reward her. Instead, he has angered Sonya who now believes that the company does not appreciate her. The real tragedy is that the bonus may well be paid in the following month when the company can better afford it. If that is the case, it means that Sonya may be angry for the delay, even if she gets the bonus next month. What was intended to be a reward has backfired to the extent that Frank has compromised his credibility.

SECTION III — The Doctor's Rx

Never Promise your associates anything, just deliver

As a rule, never make a promise you cannot keep, or that you are not empowered to keep on your own. It is impossible to know what the people higher up in an organization are thinking, or all of the factors that influence their decisions. Do not assume that the bosses are unfair; assume that they are caring and want to do the right thing. They may know something that you do not, or more importantly, the decision may be much more complex than your view allows you to understand.

Even when hiring people, it is best to avoid giving the candidates any real idea of what their next job might be. I always say "your promotions are earned and they can come whenever the performance and needs of the company coincide. Promotions are not scheduled they are earned."

SECTION IV — Ask the Doctor

Tandy: My boss recently told me that he was recommending me for a position that had opened up above me. I was so excited that after three years on the job I would finally get a promotion that I went home and told my brother and sister. Last week they took me out to dinner to celebrate. Then this morning, I got the news from my boss that I was not even a finalist and that somebody from another department had been promoted to the job. I am really upset, and I do not know what to do.

The Doctor: Tandy, I am so sorry, but you are not alone. Many people every day get passed over for promotion. Your boss did not use good judgment in telling you about the possible promotion before it was even clear if you would be considered as a finalist. Your disappointment is understandable, but you should not despair. Now that you recognize how much you want a promotion, you should be proactive in learning what you must do to earn one in the future.

I recommend that you got back to your boss and ask a few questions:

1. **Ask what the process for getting promoted is.** You mentioned that somebody from another department got the job. That indicates that the pool of candidates was larger than just your department. Is there a formal job posting system, or a formal process that requires all people at a certain level to be considered for open positions? You may have been among hundreds of eligible applicants, and some of them may have been better qualified from tenure, education, evaluations or even experience. It is also possible that your boss did not play a role in the decision process.

2. **Ask who got the job, and the key reasons for that candidate being selected.** It is important for you to determine what is required to get the next promotion, and whether your own background and performance meet those requirements. In addition, you need to know the person's background, because it may mean learn that you need to gain some other experience in a different division of the company.

3. **Ask what your boss thinks you need to do to get the next promotion.** This is critical, because it will make

your boss think about it. It is possible that she had no idea what the company wants in that job category, but if she can give you some insight then maybe she can also help you on the way to your goal.

4. **Ask what other jobs are available.** This will send a clear message that you are interested in advancement and that you want to be considered.

Most importantly, thank your boss for thinking of you and tell her that you will continue to do a great job. It is important that you show appreciation and that you do not appear angry. Your boss probably feels just as badly as you do, so being positive about the situation will help her to feel better. Remember, you want her to recommend you again.

Sammy: I just applied for a different job within my company and did not get it. What should I do?

The Doctor: I suggest that you follow the recommendation that I gave Tandy and ask questions that will help you better understand what is required to get the job you want. In addition, I have a couple of other ideas:

1. **Make certain you keep looking for job opportunities.** You are probably in a large enough company where there are many job openings. Keep trying; if you are good you will eventually hit on a job that works for you.

2. **Make certain that you are qualified.** Larger companies typically have rigorous requirements for education and experience. Make certain you know who the winners are and why they were selected over you.

3. **It is possible that just tenure alone is all that it takes.** Hang in there; focus on giving a stellar performance every day and "your time will come."

For both Tandy and Sammy: in spite of all this advice, if you continue to get "passed over" you might ultimately have to look outside your companies. It may help you to know how other employers view your skills and performance. It is possible that you will find precisely the job that you want somewhere else. I always encourage associates to seek advancement internally in their current companies, but one should not disregard the external opportunities either.

16

A Mistaken Hire

HOW MANY TIMES HAVE you interviewed, and decided to hire a person, only to realize shortly after he or she started that it was probably a mistake? I have hired hundreds, perhaps thousands of people in my career, and have learned from my mistakes. For every error I have made in my hiring decisions, I have vowed an equal number of times that I won't let it happen again. Unfortunately, I recently found myself having to renew those vows.

There are a variety of reasons we make mistaken hires, and I suspect that the aggregate of my mistakes can be attributed to the entire spectrum of those reasons. I have hired too fast because I needed somebody too much; I have hired somebody who said all the right things, but had no real track record to justify the words; I have hired somebody who moved jobs every six to 12 months, thinking this time would be the exception; I have hired somebody, in spite of my great reservations, because one of my associates thought the person was strong; I have even have hired somebody based on a friend's recommendation and I failed to do anything that approximated a real interview. The list goes on and on. Every reason is contrary to the advice that I give my clients; and yet, every once in a while, I do it again.

The reason for my recent mistaken hire is that I took a chance. I have had great results from "taking a chance" but this was not one of those times. I hired a young man who clearly had little formal educational background, and even less demonstrated work experience. I went with my "gut" rather than my head. I will admit that I have frequently gone with my gut, and have been pretty lucky that the decisions were good ones. This time my gut instincts were wrong.

This is not a story about how to do a better job hiring; it is a story about how to respond when you are faced with a potentially "mistaken hire". The core message: when you make a mistake, admit it and take immediate action to fix the problem. If a new employee is not working out as you had hoped, it is essential to act quickly in identifying the problem and helping that person get back on track to success.

In the case of the young man I recently hired, it was evident early on that he lacked some essential skills and those shortcomings were causing errors in his work performance. As the significance of those problems grew it began to take a toll on the organization. I reacted quickly and started the counseling process. I engaged my new associate in frequent counseling sessions during which I gave him direct and targeted feedback on his performance. When the problems persisted, I suggested that he give thoughtful consideration to whether this job was right for him.

Ironically, within a few days of that conversation, he came back to me and said that he agreed that he was having trouble and that some aspects of the job were not a good fit for him. His assessment of the situation led to further discussions, and ultimately we assigned him to a different job that we all hoped was a better fit and would help him succeed. We began the search for a new person to take on the young man's previous duties while we worked to transition him to the new job. Within two weeks we had hired a replacement for the first job and started the transition.

That is where the situation stood after a little more than two months of his employment. The story came to an abrupt end when the young man resigned because he was not happy in his job. This is the part of the story that has the great lesson, even for me. We had made a "mistaken hire" and we were trying very hard to help this young man find an effective place in our organization, but the problem was deeper than his lack of skills for certain aspects of the job. It is now clear to me that he was a bad fit for our organization on many levels, and we were trying to fix the wrong problem.

I wanted to salvage the hire. I wanted so much to not have made a mistake, that I was blinded to the fact that this young man may have been having performance problems simply because he did not fit in the culture of our firm. Performance problems are not always a function of the knowledge, skills and attitudes of the associates, as they can be dramatically impacted by the fact that there is a bad fit psychologically.

This young man needed to be in an organization where artistic creativity drove the organizational success, rather than high performance goals and task achievement. We have a high-energy firm, where we multitask and focus on a broad range of activities and commitments. Our creativity is channeled into program development and writing on real world topics of leadership and governance. We simply did not provide an environment where he felt comfortable because much of what we do was like a foreign language to him. The shame is on me for not recognizing that, and counseling him to find a job in a different organization. He may not have really understood the reasons, but he realized that the fit was wrong and made the decision to go. It took courage on his part, but I am convinced that it was the right thing for him and for us. In retrospect, we suspected that he would not succeed in the new job either, but we wanted to give him a second chance.

In the leadership strategy that I teach, the "Assignment" principle requires job design and description to be coupled with assigning the right person to the job. By making the wrong assignment, I have gained a better understanding of the elements of success in our organization. The culture of the organization can either be energizing or enervating, depending on how it fits with an individual's psychology. I hope that you will learn from my mistake, and be certain that the criteria you develop for a new hire include a clear understanding of how the culture of the organization impacts the people who will be hired.

SECTION II: Mini Case — "Sally Starts a New Job"

Sally had worked at the same company for the past ten years and had been very happy throughout her employment there. She had become the most senior analyst in her unit and had received several formal recognitions of her exceptional performance. She was proud of her accomplishments and work and continually sought opportunities to excel. Sally was a great employee.

One day, Sally woke up and realized that she was bored. The feeling grew over a period of several months, and eventually she concluded that it was time to make a change. She went to her boss and told him that she needed a break and wanted to do something else. Her boss said, "Sally you are the best we have in the unit, why would you want to change?" "I have been doing the same thing for ten years and I am a bit bored, please let me do something new," she said to him. "I am sorry, Sally," he said, "but

I don't have any other job to offer that you would be qualified for." Sally went home and tossed and turned all night. The next day, she went to the HR department and asked them for advice. They promised to look into the situation get back to her with some options.

Sally waited for three weeks and heard nothing. She called the HR representative for a status report and was told that they had nothing for her and that she needed to be patient. That was not what she wanted to hear, and when she went home she suffered through another restless night. She returned to work the following day and promptly resigned.

What happened, and what could have been done to avoid this event?

There are "Sallys" in every organization, and my guess is that everybody reading this has either been a Sally or had a Sally work for them. Most of us thrive on challenge and success, and are bored by the continual repetition of tasks that we have long since mastered. There is no cure for the boredom, short of a job change. The best performers, regardless of the nature of the work, will eventually be so good that they can practically do their job on autopilot. Even the CEO of a company can "burn out," from the repetition inherent in doing the same job for a long time.

Sally's company, her boss and the HR department representative in particular, blew an opportunity to keep a great, loyal employee in the organization. Maybe her boss failed to understand the boredom, or perhaps he was selfishly reluctant to help her get a new job because then he would lose a great performer. Whichever the case, the company failed.

This boss should have asked himself how he would feel after doing the same job for ten years. His answer probably would have led him to be much more aggressive in helping Sally expand her work scope. Had he thought about it, he probably could have given Sally a small project or special assignment that would have at least added something new to her activities while he explored other options for her. Every boss who loves his/her associates would respond to a situation like this by focusing on ways to help that associate achieve her goals. All organizations rely on high quality talent, which must be both nurtured and challenged.

SECTION III — The Doctor's Rx

The key to assessing how people are doing in their jobs is simple: ask. All too many of us just assume that our associates are doing fine. I know from personal experience that most people do not complain about their jobs, they simply leave when they become unhappy or unfulfilled. Make it a point to periodically ask your associates how they are doing, and let them know that you really want an honest and meaningful answer because you genuinely care.

So few people in leadership positions actually do the asking, that when you do ask in a sincere and caring manner, you may be surprised how candid and honest the response is. They key, however, is that if you get feedback that says, "I am not happy," then you must follow up by doing something about it. If you ask but fail to respond according to the answer, then you will never again get an honest answer, and are likely to end up with a "Sally" termination.

SECTION IV — Ask the Doctor

David: I have followed your advice and asked my associates if they are happy. One employee said "No, I am not happy because I do not like working for you." What do I do now?

The Doctor: Well, when you ask that question, you need to be prepared for almost anything, including a personal attack. You now know that you are perceived as the problem by this particular individual, and the burden has shifted to you. I have also heard this response on more than one occasion. The first time you get that kind of feedback can be a shock.

Recognize that you may or may not be the problem. Just because your associate says that, does not mean you are. This person simply may not be able to accept the organizational expectations, or he may find that his assignment does not fit his capabilities. It may be easier for him to blame his inadequacy on you rather than to take the responsibility himself. If that is the case, you need to help this individual accept the mismatch and then take the necessary action to help him improve or "move on."

On the other hand, you should not disregard the possibility that you are the problem. It takes a pretty secure personality to accept the allegation and to be introspective enough to assess it fairly. As I said, I have had that answer more than once, and I will admit that there were a couple of times when it was clear to me that I was the problem. Whether it was a bad day, or even a series of bad days, I had failed to be the "understanding" boss I pride myself in being. You need to be honest with yourself and second guess your own behavior. Remember that when you have a bad day, your staff has a bad day. Take a critical look at yourself, but also go back to that associate and ask him to tell you precisely what he thinks your problem is. Listen carefully, and process the answers. By engaging in an "unemotional" dialogue it may help you, and him, find the real cause of the frustration and pain.

Week 3

LEAD

DAY 17

ASSIGNMENT

"SQUARE PEGS IN Round Holes Never Fit!"

If you follow the ten steps in my book, <u>Lead with Love</u>, you will notice that there seems to be a sequential nature to these steps. Life, and certainly leadership, is not always linear or sequential, but there is some logic to thinking about the process in something of a sequential manner. There is little doubt in my mind that starting with the right mind set—Love—is an essential starting point. You probably agree that setting the expectations for the unit and the individual jobs is a logical first step in the journey toward having a productive work unit. The next step we outline, Assignment, is equally logical as the next step in our sequence. Once you decide what needs to be done (Expectations) as a unit leader, you obviously need to determine how it is going to get done and who is going to do it (Assignment).

Assignment is a critical to your goal of being a peak performance leader, because without the proper structure for doing a job and the proper assignment of staff to that job, there is not much that you will be able to accomplish regardless of your efforts and intentions. Your staff members must have the core characteristics that the job requires for success. No amount of training or leading on your part will be able to make a worker succeed in a job where he or she simply does not fit.

When you staff your team in the world of work, you must make clear decisions about what the job requires and what the person will need to do. Then you have to match that set of requirements with the right talent. Selecting the right people will at least give you a fair chance at achieving your goals. Without the right knowledge, skills, attitudes and work experience, your staff will undoubtedly fail.

Choosing the right people for the job is one of the toughest tasks you will be asked to execute as a leader. The recruitment, employment and placement of the right people is both an "art" and a "science." There are many right and wrong ways to go about hiring your staff, but rest assured that success is not guaranteed on every hire. You will make mistakes (just as I have many times over the years) but you should try to learn from your wrong choices in order to improve your ability in hiring. Every wrong hire is far more expensive than the out-of-pocket costs associated with attracting and processing a new hire. The loss is even greater when you consider the cost of turnover when the hire fails.

The key to effective hiring is effective interviewing, and the key to effective interviews is to use your ears and brain, not your mouth and vocal chords. My most important advice to you for interviewing candidates is to listen to *their answers*, not *your questions*. You may ask the right question but still come away with a bad decision if you fail to listen carefully to the response. You must process the answer as a piece of information that you can use to evaluate the capabilities of the candidate. All of that said, interviewing takes practice and a solid understanding of human behavior. If you can get help in the form of formal training, take it. It will probably pay huge dividends for you.

SECTION II: Mini Case — The World's Shortest Interview

Tammy was about to start the interview when it occurred to her that she did not have the candidate's resume. She hurriedly looked through several files, but then had to give up because Kyle had arrived for the interview and was waiting for her in the conference room. Out of time, Tammy went to the conference room to do the interview. "Hello Kyle," Tammy said, as she walked in and extended her hand to shake Kyle's. Kyle muttered a hello, and following the hand shake he sat down as soon as Tammy did.

"Kyle, I've misplaced your resume, do you have a copy?" Tammy asked. Kyle was caught off guard and said, "No, I forgot to bring one." Tammy told him not to worry, that they could proceed without it. "Tell me," she began "why do you want to work at Acme?" Kyle was a little surprised by the question, but answered, "Well, I use your products and I think that your benefit programs will give me an opportunity to work on a graduate degree. After that, I don't know what I want to do. Are there a lot of chances to move up the ladder at Acme?"

Tammy was not overly impressed with his answer, but she told him that she understood how difficult it can be to think about the future. "How do you plan to use the degree to further your career?" she asked.

"Well, I am convinced that the people with graduate degrees are going to get the best jobs. I want to get a graduate degree while I'm young so that I can leverage it for that much longer," Kyle replied.

"What are you planning to study in graduate school?" asked Tammy.

"Well, I don't know, but it's not going to be accounting-related. I don't like accounting at all," he said. "I think that I can get an MBA in sales and marketing, which is an area that should be a real advantage for me in the job market. Tammy was now convinced that she knew enough, and would hire Kyle because he was smart, ambitious and immediately available. Filling the job quickly is a priority for Tammy, and she is certain that Kyle has all the tools to be successful. She thanked him and told him she would get back to him the next day.

Question: How would you score the interview? The interviewer? The candidate?

Answer: Obviously, the interview has been shortened to allow room for this discussion, but honestly, I give it a failing score. Both Tammy and Kyle performed dismally, and the interview was essentially a bust. Her questions led immediately to the subject of graduate school, rather than the critical information about his knowledge, skills and attitudes. She learned nothing about what Kyle has done or even could do. In light of the fact that she also didn't have his resume at hand, it seems that all Tammy knows about Kyle is that he wants to go to graduate school and study something.

Kyle has learned nothing about the job, and the only thing that he has revealed about himself is that he wants to go to graduate school. His unusually honest admission that he doesn't know what he wants to study is unnerving, because it suggests that he hasn't even thought about it. His negativity about accounting may be a red flag that he can't deal with numbers, which are the bottom line of most companies. In short, neither party performed well nor learned much of anything.

One crucial mistake that Tammy makes shows up at the very end of the case. She obviously has a major hole in her organization and thinks that she must fill it immediately. This is perhaps the biggest mistake that you can make as a leader who is in the Assignment phase of leading. Remember that making a bad hire to just fill a hole is worse than leaving the hole. Never hire a "body" to fill a hole in your organization. It will always be a costly mistake.

SECTION III — The Doctor's Rx

The interview can be a great tool or simply a waste of time. It is essential that you manage the interview, and that you get your agenda covered in the time you have. Some tips for solid interviews:

1. Leave enough time to learn something substantial about the candidate. A 15 minute interview is going to be useless; allow at least an hour.
2. Make certain that you and the candidate can be comfortable. Neither should want the interview to end quickly just because the chair is uncomfortable.
3. Avoid questions that have a yes or no answer. Structure the questions so that the candidate needs to think and respond with more than one sentence.
4. Ask questions that focus on things that the person did, not things that they might do. You are trying find out what they did, not what they think you might want to hear as the "ideal answer."
5. Make certain you give the candidate a chance to ask you questions. You can learn a lot about the candidate from the questions asked.
6. Do not telegraph to the candidate in the first interview that you are going to hire them. You need time to consider the fit, as do they.

7. Get references, and check them. There are constraints on what people can say, but you need to talk to people who know the candidate. Avoid their friends; find bosses.
8. Take notes
9. Listen, Listen, Listen

SECTION IV — Ask the Doctor

Gloria: I have 12 people who report to me. One of the 12 has been demoted from an intern down. This person is bitter about the demotion, but he is performing up to standard. Every now and then he expresses his opinion that he is more qualified to be a manager than existing managers. He is paranoid. Anytime he receives non favorable reviews or comments about himself, he states that this is a plot to fire him. Anytime something is not what he believes it should be, he wants to grieve the situation. Most of the time his grieving is in vain because he has overlooked important information.

What are your suggestions on managing this type of person?

The Doctor: When people get "demoted" they almost always get "demotivated." That is without question what has happened to your associate. Indeed, the paranoid view of the world is pretty predictable. I think if you put yourself into the same situation, it is pretty clear that you would not be a happy camper. In fact, your associate is probably not paranoid; he is probably correct. By that I mean: something serious must have been found in his behavior or performance for him to have been demoted. Assuming it was serious enough to demote, but not serious enough to fire, then he is probably convinced that the next shoe to drop is for him to lose his job.

But all of that does not answer your question. The first thing you need to do, is to be certain that you are behaving in a fair and objective way about his performance. Since I do not know from your question what caused the demotion, I can only assume that you did not cause it to happen and may even have inherited this associate. Whatever caused his demotion, he has now been punished and it is imperative that you treat his work objectively.

On the other hand, he is not making it easy for you to deal with the situation. Although I am assuming you have already talked to him about his behavior, my guess is you have not been very direct. Unless, and until, his performance deteriorates, or he actually has a negative impact on your other staff members, I would suggest you give him time to get through the healing process. He has taken a body blow and you need to give him time to get the grieving out of his system. If it does not slow down, or if it gets worse, then you are going to need to take some action.

Obviously, you need to follow your organization's policies and procedures for progressive feedback and documentation, but my suggestion would be to go beyond that. If there is any reason for you to believe that you or your other staff members are being "blamed" for his demotion then he may become an unhealthy element in the group. If he does not eventually seem to be "getting over it", then you need to consider trying to find him another job in your organization where he does not have all the memories and constant reminders of his failure. This guy may be a serious problem to you, but if he cannot heal his anger, he will be a serious problem for himself as well.

One last thought, if your organization has an Employee Assistance Program, you might want to consider getting him to take advantage of some of that counseling help. He clearly needs to get over his anger, so you should try to help him in any way you can...that is until he fails to do his job. Then, you have a duty to your staff to deal with the performance issue.

DAY 18

COMMIT TO COMMUNICATING

MY BOOKSHELF IS FILLED with books on leadership, because it is important to continually remind myself of lessons I have learned, study the strategies of other leaders, and continue to grow and develop my own leadership abilities. Two books that I recently read focus on a topic that is critical for leaders: the art of communication. *Words That Work* by Dr. Frank Luntz and *Words That Change Minds* by Shelle Rose Charvet both impart the message that language is an incredibly powerful tool that can make the difference between winning and losing, success and failure. Leaders who want to influence, motivate and win must communicate effectively.

In *Words That Work*, Luntz focuses on how language is perceived, as he believes "it's not what you say, it's what people hear" that matters. He is an acclaimed wordsmith and communicator, serving as an advisor to CEOs of large corporations, as well as politicians, advocacy groups and world leaders. A testament to his art of manipulating perception is the fact that he coined the emotionally charged phrase "death tax" to replace the politically benign "estate tax", and turned the negative connotation of "drilling for oil" into a positive act with the phrase "exploring for energy." In his book, Lutz uses case studies from high profile corporations and political campaigns to demonstrate that the key to communication is in understanding how the person on the receiving end will interpret your message based on their own emotions, beliefs, assumptions and biases.

Whether, you want to close a deal, get a raise or influence your staff, your language should be tailored to your listener's point of view. In my work as a consultant and public speaker, I work with a wide variety of professionals that range from boards of directors and chief executives to low and mid-level managers. Communicating effectively to those diverse groups requires that I adjust my language accordingly, as my message would not be received if I failed to consider the differences in those audiences. Leaders at all levels communicate with associates, customers, vendors and others who have very different views and backgrounds. Those who tailor their language to fit the audience are much more likely to make an impact.

Luntz offers "10 Rules of Effective Language" as a guide to successful communication. His rules seem simple and obvious, yet he points out that all of the best advertising taglines (the words that stick in our brains and spur us to take action) all abide by these rules. Following are his rules, as well as familiar slogans that demonstrate words that work:

1. **Simplicity: Use Small Words** – "I'm lovin' it" (McDonald's); "Snap, Crackle, Pop" (Kellogg)
2. **Brevity: Use Short Sentences** – "Have it your way" (Burger King); "Just do it" (Nike)
3. **Credibility: Is as Important as Philosophy** – "You're in good hands" (Allstate); "Nothing runs like a Deere" (John Deere)
4. **Consistency Matters** - "Always Low Prices. Always" (Wal-Mart) "It keeps going, and going and going" (Energizer)
5. **Novelty: Offer Something New** – "Think Outside the Bun" (Taco Bell); "No more tears" (Johnson & Johnson)
6. **Sound and Texture Matter** – "M'm! M'm! Good!" (Campbell's); "Fill it to the rim with Brim" (Brim coffee)
7. **Speak Aspirationally** – "Be all you can be" (US Army); "Like a Good Neighbor" (State Farm)
8. **Visualize** – "Let your fingers do the walking" (Yellow Pages); "Finger lickin' good" (KFC)
9. **Ask a Question** - "What's in your wallet?" (Capital One); "Got Milk?" (Milk)
10. **Provide Context and Explain Relevance** – "Because I'm worth it" (L'Oreal); "When you care enough to send the very best" (Hallmark)

Most of us aren't responsible for creating slogans that establish a brand identity for our organizations or the products we offer; however, the simplicity and impact of the most memorable slogans demonstrates that good communication isn't complicated. Short and simple works. Luntz advises using accessible language that connects to ideas, emotions, hopes, and fears. In Words That Change Minds, Charvet takes this same concept of language that motivates people, and then applies it to behavior patterns and triggers. Her book is a more complex approach to communication, but the bottom line for both authors is that language is our most powerful tool for success.

SECTION II: Mini Case — Inbox Overload

Ryan had recently graduated college and was not really sure what he wanted to do with his career. He thought he wanted to work in finance, and that he should get an MBA, but he needed a little experience, as well as to save some money for tuition, before he committed himself to that path. In the meantime, he had taken a position as the Executive Assistant to the CEO of a successful private equity firm in hopes of gaining experience and knowledge of the industry. The CEO, Wayne, recognized after just three months that Ryan had a lot of potential and began mentoring him towards becoming a Junior Associate.

At first Ryan was thrilled with his progress and prospects for advancement. Now, six months into the job, he is ready to quit. In addition to the demands of organizing his boss's busy travel schedule, scheduling meetings and other administrative duties, he is being inundated with information about the other associates' and executives' correspondence, negotiations, and deals. Due to the fact that his boss travels so often, most of the information comes via email, and Ryan can't keep up with the steady torrent into his inbox, let alone stay on top of all of his assignments as an executive assistant.

Feeling overwhelmed, he asked to meet with his boss face to face and told him about his struggle to get his work done due to the flood of email. Wayne said "Ryan, this is the most efficient way for me to communicate and you simply have to adapt. I think you have great potential and would like to see you advance in our firm, but that means you have to find a balance so that you can accomplish your work as well as handle the email correspondence." Ryan left the meeting completely dejected. He sincerely wanted to become a Junior Associate at the firm, yet he felt that he was suffering death by email. His boss's response had done nothing to make him believe that the circumstances would change, and he was contemplating whether he should quit.

Should Ryan "adapt" or move on?

Based on the information provided, it appears that Wayne is a good boss who has determined that Ryan has the talent and ability to merit a promotion. Furthermore, he is mentoring him and providing him the information he needs to advance. Ryan clearly wants to be promoted, and has been given a good opportunity with his current employer. All of this suggests that Ryan should adapt, and learn how to be productive and simultaneously handle the emails.

The ease of access, ability to communicate from remote locations and instantaneous delivery are just a few of the advantages of email. Wayne would probably not be nearly as productive if he couldn't communicate with his staff via email, particularly in light of his travel schedule. Ryan must accept this fact, and find a way to handle emails and remain productive. The lesson that Ryan needs to learn is from the first chapter in my book You're in Charge…What Now which is the "The Law of Administrivia".

The Law of Administrivia postulates that… *Required or less useful activity drives out desirable and useful activity.* In other words, people will do the tasks that they think are easy, trivial, and required first, in order to get them out of the way. Then, with the time left over, they will do what is desirable or useful but not required. The amount of trivial administrative tasks (administrivia) tends to grow once the boss concludes you are able to handle what you have already been given to accomplish.

Eventually you do less and less of what you want or need to do and much more of the administrative work.

When Ryan reads the email in his inbox, he should quickly skim through them and determine which ones require immediate attention and action. The emails that can wait should be saved and read when he has accomplished the work that he really needs to do. This may require that he take the emails that he set aside home with him in the evening or over the weekend, but if he wants to succeed in this organization, he has to work at the pace established by his superiors.

Although this case doesn't address email etiquette, it is important to point out that the ease and speed of email make many people become lazy and careless when emailing. A leader should always communicate professionally, and that includes using complete sentences, proper grammar and spell check when sending emails. Even if the correspondence is a simple exchange with an associate, the leader sets the standard that others will follow. If a leader is sloppy in email communication, that sloppiness will be reflected in the associates' communication with clients and customers.

SECTION III — The Doctor's Rx

A common understanding in the art of sales is that the person who asks the questions controls the conversation. The more answers you get, the more knowledge and understanding you have about a prospect's needs. The same philosophy can be applied to leadership and explains why great leaders are invariably great listeners. Communication is not merely the act of telling others your point of view, and having that message properly understood. For leaders, effective communication requires more listening than telling. By asking your associates questions, and listening to their responses, you learn where your employees need development, and you benefit from their individual ideas and knowledge. Here are a few tips on being a better listener:

- Maintain eye contact. We've all experienced the frustration of trying to talk to someone while they look around the room, or even worse, continue working. This behavior demonstrates a lack of interest or concern for what the person has to say. Show genuine respect and interest by keeping your gaze fixed on the person who is talking.

- Ask questions. Do not wait for your associates to come to you and volunteer their thoughts, opinions and challenges. Only by posing questions yourself, and listening to the answers, can you be assured of where things stand. When you receive an answer, ask a follow-up question so that you can gain more information and insight. This also shows that you are listening, and care about their answers.

- Give feedback. Associates actually want to know how they are doing and where they can improve. By giving frequent feedback, you and your associates will know if they are on track for reaching the organization's goals. It also allows you to correct undesirable behavior before it is "too late".

- Ask the tough questions. A willingness to delve into difficult issues creates a trust and openness that will be of benefit to you and your associates. Among the "toughest" questions to ask is for their feedback on how you are doing as a leader. Don't avoid this one, as self-assessment and continuing development are part of your role as a leader.

SECTION IV — Ask the Doctor

Stephanie: I was so glad to read about the National Leadership Institute and your involvement in training nonprofit organizations. I serve on a nonprofit committee and have just been nominated to be the chair for the coming year. My committee is responsible for one of the organization's fundraisers, and I really want to be a good leader and surpass our goals. In my experience on the committee this year, I was frustrated during meetings because the chair let people chatter on and on, and derail us from the business on the agenda. Our meetings always went over the allotted time, and I think that explains why most members attended meetings on a very irregular basis.

When I am the chair, I want to stick to the agenda and timeframe, which I hope will improve attendance. My concern is that I will come across as too strict or businesslike, and alienate people whom I understand are volunteering their time. How do I keep the meetings professional, and yet not hurt feelings or offend those who are talking too long or out of turn?

The Doctor: Helping nonprofit leadership to achieve excellence is a passion of mine, and the reason for which I founded the National Leadership Institute. For the last 25 years I have volunteered and served on the boards of diverse nonprofit organizations, so I empathize with and understand your concerns. I also admire the fact that you have reached out for guidance as it says to me that you are truly committed to being a good leader and furthering the goals of your organization.

In your email, you (perhaps unknowingly) identified two characteristics of nonprofits that differ from traditional businesses. The first is that your "workers" are volunteers. People join nonprofits for a variety of reasons that include socializing, business networking and helping a particular cause. Because they are volunteering their time, and attendance is not mandatory for a paycheck or other necessity, committee members' sense of responsibility for meetings and commitments will vary. The second characteristic is that time is a critical issue. Most volunteers have jobs, family, personal interests and other demands that make "free time" both limited and precious. If you want to keep your committee engaged and involved, you must be sensitive to the fact that they are sacrificing time that could be spent on other activities.

My recommendations to you are as follows:

If you have not already done so, read <u>Robert's Rules of Order</u> which is a guide that spells out parliamentary procedure and is widely used by nonprofits for proper conduct during meetings. Your organization or committee may not require the formality of these rules, but there are great tips for keeping meetings orderly and on track.

Second, the key to your success will be communication. Your plan to stick to the agenda during meetings is absolutely the right approach. Respecting the amount of time set aside for a meeting, and getting through the business at hand are critical for continual participation and progress. Before each meeting, prepare an agenda with all of the items that will be covered, as well as the time allotted for presenters and discussion of each item. Provide a copy of the agenda to each committee member well in advance of the meeting, and ask them to propose any issues that they think need to be included. Remind them that only items on the agenda will be discussed at the upcoming meeting. Plan to set your personal time aside at the end of each meeting to discuss individual questions and issues that were not on the agenda, as well as to be social with those who have more time and want to talk with you. Personal connections often make the difference in how much time or energy a person is willing to give, so you have a critical role in fostering relationships with your committee members.

When you begin each meeting, pass out a copy of the agenda and tell your committee how much you appreciate their time and participation. Following that, ask for their cooperation in staying on track so that the meeting concludes in a timely manner. If you communicate kindly but with authority, they will understand that you are leading with their best interests in mind. Nevertheless, "talkers" will inevitably put your meetings off track if not handled properly. Keep in mind that those who share ideas and ask questions may have valid points that need to be addressed, so "talkers" are often a great asset. When a person veers off of the business at hand, interrupt politely and reiterate that you want to adhere to the agenda based on everyone's time constraints, but that the discussion could continue after the meeting or be added as an agenda item for the next meeting.

It is important that your language and communication remains positive and that you avoid saying something that can be interpreted as negative or discouraging. To handle a sidetrack with sensitivity, say something encouraging such as "That's a really good idea and I would love to have you do a summary of your thoughts and suggestions so that I can send it to the committee and add it to the agenda for discussion at the next meeting. Let's talk after we adjourn, so that those who need to leave aren't running late." Another good tactic is humor. I know a school teacher who chairs a nonprofit committee and jokingly applies the same tactics to her committee members that she does to her students when they're not paying attention. I wouldn't be able to pull that off, but we all have a personal style of humor that can be applied to soften the "strict" job of being a leader.

I wish you the best of luck in your new leadership role, and encourage you to contact the National Leadership Institute if you need further guidance or training. You may be on track for a board position, and if so, I recommend that you read my book <u>You're a Non-Profit Director...What Now?</u>.

TRUE PASSION DRIVES BEHAVIOR AND CREATES WINNING PERFORMANCE

IF YOU HAVE EVER BEEN a sports fan, you know about the power of Passion. In sports, it is typically called emotion. You can see how emotion (passion) impacts the outcome of sports almost every time you participate in, or observe the flow of a game. The success or failure of most teams is also impacted by the natural capabilities, knowledge and skills of the players, but the end result of competition is driven much more by emotion. Most of the teams in the National Football League (NFL) or the National Basketball Association (NBA) are well-balanced with players of comparable skills. There are a few exceptions such as the phenomenal quarterbacks Bret

Farve and Payton Manning, basketball giant Shaquile O'Neil and superstar Michael Jordan, but by and large, on any given day any team could win.

The obvious differentiator is the role of emotion, and in sports, that emotion usually increases the amount of adrenalin flowing. Coaches encourage this by "pumping up" their teams with emotional speeches. The players then sustain that emotion with screams and enthusiastic celebrations at every success. Their emotions may stem from anger at the foe, anger at the prospect of losing, fear of the coach's anger or even excitement at the prospect of winning. Whatever the emotion, when the team is "pumped up," they often win, regardless, of their skill level. It is not always the better team that wins, but rather the team that has the highest emotional investment.

In the world of work, emotion does not play precisely the same type of role, but it plays a role nonetheless. It is seldom the reality that the work team is infused with huge amounts of emotion induced adrenaline, but emotion does generate a new kind of reaction. The difference is that in the world of work, we are not limited to 60 minutes of playing time. Instead, we are expected to sustain our passion over an extended period of time. Raw emotion which generates the adrenaline rush cannot be sustained, so in the work place, we must have a substantially different mechanism to drive performance that exceeds the norm, and expected level of success. In this case, the better term to define emotional impact is passion. Passion plays the same type of role in the world of work that adrenaline plays in sports. In order to achieve sustained winning performance, we must have the passion to achieve outstanding performance.

So what is passion? The dictionary offers a variety of definitions:

1. Any powerful or compelling emotion or feeling, as love or hate.
2. Strong amorous feeling or desire; love; ardor.
3. Strong sexual desire; lust.
4. An instance or experience of strong love or sexual desire.
5. A person toward whom one feels strong love or sexual desire.
6. A strong or extravagant fondness, enthusiasm, or desire for anything: a passion for music.
7. The object of such a fondness or desire: Accuracy became a passion with him.
8. An outburst of strong emotion or feeling: He suddenly broke into a passion of bitter words.
9. Violent anger.

Obviously, the definitions focused on sexual desire, are not the relevant definition, but further down we have the key to understanding the type of passion we need in the world of work… a strong or extravagant fondness, enthusiasm, or desire for anything: a passion for music. In the case of an employee, it is a passion to live by the organization's values and to achieve the organization's goals.

That does not tell the whole story. Passion is something that we feel in our psyche, or in our soul. It is an emotion deep inside us that says "I believe so much in the core values and goals, that I will not let anything stop me from pursuing and achieving those goals." It is an emotion that is driven from belief, not a belief driven from emotion or from adrenaline. This type of motivation to achieve is uniquely human and reflects the best in us as members of our species.

Our passion to win is not enough; we must have the passion to achieve the goals of the organization. Achieving a winning record as a leader requires a passion that that drives us to perform exceptionally and to exceed goals. Passion is the work life equivalent of adrenaline in sports. There is no doubt that a belief in the core values of an organization can energize us to further those beliefs, but only a passion to achieve organizational goals can drive us to achieve what to some will seem like the impossible.

SECTION II: Mini Case — The Lost Promotion

Sandy has been a Director of Administration for three years and has a thirst for success. She started at her company, a strategy consulting organization, with the express intention of becoming a strategy consultant. Everyone in her family had worked as a consultant, and her youngest brother had just been hired by a premier consulting organization when Sandy took her current job. It was expected that Sandy would some day be a consultant as well.

Sandy is very bright and excelled in high school and college. School had always been pretty easy for her, but because she had many talents, choosing a college major was perhaps a tough decision. She finally decided at the last minute, and graduated with a B.A. in fine arts. Given that major, Sandy realized that she realized that she was not going to be hired as a consultant straight out of school, so she took the administrative manager job at her current firm, with the clear objective of working her way into a consulting position.

Since she started at the firm, Sandy made her goals known. It was no secret that she was not interested in staying in the administrative services part of the firm. The irony was that Sandy was really good at her job. Much of the learning that she did in college actually paid off for her. She had a great artistic flair and her influence over the collateral materials projects had been significant. The marketing department consistently relied on her advice about formatting, and graphic design whenever they had a new materials project.

Unfortunately, after three years at the firm, Sandy had not yet been considered for a strategy consulting assignment. Every time she brought it up with her boss, she got the answer, "Not yet Sandy. You are doing such a great job where you are, we need you right there." Sandy would walk away with mixed emotions. She knew she was doing a great job, and actually she really enjoyed many aspects of her work. On the other hand, she was frustrated at the lack of progress toward her goal. Whenever she asked why she could not get a consulting assignment, the answer usually included also something about her lack of education in the field.

Today is the day of Sandy's performance appraisal. She hopes it will also be the day when she learns about the timeframe on her transition to being a consultant. The company has just lost a junior consultant and that they needed to fill the void quickly, so she is confident that today is her day. During the performance review session with her boss, she is given the highest rating possible, and a salary increase that is merit-based on her outstanding performance. Then her boss says that she had been considered to fill the open consulting position, but that he and others had not recommended her because they do not believe that she is the right person for the job.

Sandy is devastated by the news and realizes that she is unlikely to ever work as a consultant in this firm. Now what should she do?

What should Sandy do?

Sandy needs to look inside herself. From what little we know, Sandy may desire that consulting job, but it is not clear that she has the Passion to get it, let alone succeed at it. It actually seems as though Sandy has more passion for her current job than she does for the one she wants. There may be some complex reasons for her expressed desire to be a strategy consultant. It is possible that the family pressure to be a consultant drives her to want that job. After three years of being told that she did not have the right education, it seems reasonable that a person with real "passion" for being a strategy consultant would start taking courses at night to add to her educational credentials. The real thirst for learning the skills seems to be missing. All that she seems to have is a "mindset" that she needs to be a consultant.

In some ways Sandy is already a "consultant" to the marketing department on graphics design. Her fine arts degree seems to have had a significant impact on her. Even though she made a last minute decision to select that field of study for her degree, it may be that she really has more passion for artistic work than she does for strategy consulting. My suggestion to Sandy is to do an honest self evaluation of her strengths and weaknesses, and to focus on becoming passionate about being great at what she loves to do, rather than what she thinks she should do.

SECTION III — The Doctor's Rx

Ask yourself if these apply to you. If your answer to many of these is no, then perhaps you need to consider whether there is a different job or organization in which you would be passionate:

- Do you gladly go to work early or leave late in order to excel?
- Do you frequently review your expectations and goals to make sure that you are on track to meet them - and then beat them?
- Are you motivated more by the pleasure of your work than by the amount of your paycheck?
- Do you seek out ways to create enthusiasm and drive in your coworkers?

- Would your coworkers describe you as dedicated to the organization and its bottom line?
- Do you truly believe in the mission and goals of the organization?
- Do you love most aspects of your work?
- Are you optimistic that you can achieve the goals that are set for you, even if they are a big step above the status quo?
- Do you spend some of your free time doing things such as reading or networking in order to enhance or improve your job performance?
- Is this your dream job?

These questions are not easy, and require you to be honest with yourself. If you are not passionate about your work, you are lacking a key ingredient for success. Since success is the reward for hard work, it makes sense to find a job that brings out your passion.

SECTION IV — Ask the Doctor

Barry: I am truly passionate about my values and believe that all of us need to help the less fortunate. I give a great deal of my time to the church and to community organizations. Unfortunately, I work for a company that does not believe we have an obligation to do anything for the poor. Our company contributions go to the symphony and opera, not to the Red Cross or Salvation Army. It really bothers me and I don't know what to do. Is this passion so important that I should quit and find another company, or should I stick it out and just live with the problem?

The Doctor: You are right to second-guess whether you and this organization are a good fit. Your passion to help the poor matters a great deal to you, and it is truly great that you act on it through your volunteer work. I encourage you to continue, as it is critical in our society that we have public and private efforts to help those less fortunate.

It sounds like your company has decided that helping the disenfranchised is not its responsibility. That may be the case, or you may not actually know what the company policy really is. I think you should take the time to ask the management precisely what their position is on that issue. If, once you get the answer, you conclude that you do not like the company perspective on this issue, then you should consider leaving. But please, make certain that you evaluate all the values of the company because it is almost impossible for you to find any company where there is not at least one issue that conflicts with your own view or opinion.

20

BEGIN EVERY ACTION WITH A COMMITMENT TO INTEGRITY

ONE OF THE KEY principles in the LEADERSHIP mnemonic is Integrity. After many years of working with a broad range of companies, I have concluded that those of us who are "In Charge" must maintain a serious focus on integrity if we are to succeed as leaders. Our society's standards of integrity have diminished to the extent that we no longer have true respect within and among our various constituencies.

Mutual respect and trust are fundamental to all human relationships. Without trust, our relationships with customers, shareholders, associates and vendors will be difficult to sustain. When there is a basic level of trust, the parties to a business relationship behave very differently than when that trust does not exist. Trust allows us to have enjoyable and efficient relationships as we pursue our organizational goals.

At the heart of trust is the commitment from every individual in an organization to behave in ways that are guided by a commitment to integrity. Our conduct must adhere at all times to the highest moral principles and professional standards. Truth, honesty and fairness are not optional, they are mandatory. It may be challenging and occasionally unpleasant, but behaving with integrity is the only way to build trust and achieve success. Integrity, and the trust that it inspires, provide great comfort to those who have business relationships with us. A breach of integrity forces our business partners to rely on testing and other controls that would be unnecessary if they had implicit trust in our behavior.

Leaders must build relationships that are founded on a commitment to integrity. Unfortunately, our society makes that commitment very difficult. It appears, even to the casual observer, that standards of integrity in our society have changed dramatically over the years. Under the traditional rules of early America, integrity was a core value of the society. Those were the days when a handshake or verbal commitment would be honored. Some believe that the secularization of our society has diminished the impact of the moral and ethical standards established by the commitment to a religious belief. The "absolute truth" standard seems to have given way to the more "nuanced" view that answers are not simply right or wrong, but rather much more "gray." The transparence of our society, with the media constantly watching and listening to every word, has caused politicians to avoid "telling it like it is" and opt instead to "spin the truth." Most of us are so accustomed to political "spin" that we seldom expect the words we hear to be a fully accurate reflection of the truth. A true commitment to integrity would require that we never "spin" anything.

Some argue that one breach of integrity by a leader can destroy any trust the associates might have. Others argue that it is our ongoing pattern of behavior that determines how we are perceived. There is no doubt some people find it difficult to accept any misjudgment which they perceive to be a breach of integrity.

Leaders must balance their commitment to integrity and their commitment to love. Often leaders tell substantially less than the "whole truth" so as to avoid jeopardizing the psychological well-being of one of their associates. In the guise of caring and sensitivity, leaders will mask the full, candid and potentially hurtful truth when communicating with their associates. Such caring is not love, and it often stems from fear that the truth will have painful consequences.

Fear can influence a leader's willingness to be candid or direct with associates during discussions about their performance. Leaders may fear reprisal from their associates; or they may be concerned that their associates have legitimate reason to question, doubt or even aggressively challenge the accuracy of the observations. How many times have you as a leader provided feedback to an individual and found the subsequent conversation more painful than it would have been had you remained silent? Leaders who have this sort of experience may try to avoid these difficult conversations in the future. In so doing, they fail to effectively lead their associates and the organization. If an associate does not receive your honest feedback, whether positive or negative, the result is that the associate is being lead with anxiety rather than love. The loving thing to do is to provide feedback that will help your associates find ways to improve their performance or behaviors.

An entire organization suffers when leaders fail to have candid, direct and meaningful conversations with their associates. Organizational performance reflects the sum total of the individual performers in the organization. The leader is ultimately accountable for the quality of that performance. When a leader fails to provide meaningful feedback that is truly of the highest integrity, the organization is cheated of the potential for improved performance. Excellence cannot be achieved without the commitment to continually improving each individual's performance. It is the leader's responsibility to use every leadership tool available to maximize the performance against expectations set by the organization and by its leaders. Leaders who have the highest standards of integrity understand this obligation to the organization and irrespective of their contemplated fears will commit to taking high integrity actions.

SECTION II: Mini Case — Martha Forgets

Martha is the Vice President of Operations at a start-up technology company headquartered in Silicon Valley. She has had several jobs in the software industry and has actually held similar positions in two other start-ups. One turned out to be a true success; the other was a complete bust. Much of the latter experience was very unpleasant, and she knows that it left scars which have yet to fully heal. She invested a good deal of money into the second company and within 18 months, the company closed its doors. Adding insult to injury, she discovered that the company's CEO had lied to virtually every investor about the state of the company, and was essentially a fraud who squandered most of the cash invested by the venture capital firms.

Martha was devastated by the experience and swore that she would never again make that type of mistake. She committed to researching the principles in her next firm, and did just that before accepting her current position. She spent a good deal of time talking to people who had worked with, and for, the current CEO and she was convinced that he was of the highest integrity.

Martha signed on about ten months ago, and she put her full energy into the job. She hired many of the same people who had worked for her at the previous "failed firm" and felt that she had assembled a great team. The company had a vision that was very similar to that of her last company, so it was easy for her to be excited, and to recruit those who had been great employees at the previous company.

Over the last three months, Martha developed serious reservations about her current CEO. There were subtle (but to her mind, clear) signs that he was making expenditures on wasteful and self-serving trips, equipment and even what she saw as personal "lifestyle perks." She was not in a position to be monitoring expense patterns, but she was convinced that money was misused in a way that reminded her of what she had seen in the last company.

Martha knew the CFO of her company pretty well, and about a month ago she decided to mention her concerns to him. After her conversation (which she pleaded he keep confidential), she had an uneasy feeling that the CFO was not very receptive to her anxiety. Her fears were then quickly confirmed when she was called into the office of the CEO and confronted with her "allegations." The meeting was pretty heated and by the time it was over, she found herself "repenting" and apologizing to the CEO for even the hint of distrust.

Since that meeting, her relationship with the CEO had clearly changed, and Martha found herself distanced from much of the core decision making. She also had several more experiences that reinforced her concerns that the CEO was not being an effective steward of the investors' money. She has now had concluded that the situation will damage the company, but she feels terribly uncertain and conflicted as to what her next step should be.

Question: Martha is at a crossroads, what should she do?

Martha has every reason to feel conflicted. From what we know, there is an overwhelmingly strong case for her to be certain that there are spending improprieties. On the other hand, her previous experience has made her understandably "gun shy" about the warning signs she sees. It is not clear that she has enough evidence to go forward with an allegation of impropriety or fraud; it is clear that she has very few options: 1) Do nothing, meaning stay and ignore the problem 2) Find another job and resign 3) Stay, and continue to monitor the behavior of the CEO, even conduct her own "investigation" 4) Report her findings to one or more members of the board of directors and/or investors.

The first option is unfortunately the one that many people take. This is tragic because it means that the individual has essentially "condoned" the behavior, as well as sacrificed their individual sense of integrity. I do not support that action because it is one of the reasons why so many of corporate America's scandals went unstopped. Too many times, the employees knew that something was wrong, yet they did nothing about it.

The second option is clearly a possibility. If the environment at the company makes the employee uncomfortable, then an action to eliminate that discomfort is reasonable. In this case, Martha tried to alert the financial control point and that failed to produce a reasonable result. It would be easy to understand if Martha decided that the best course of action for her would be to move on before the company "blows up."

The third action, or some version of it, is probably the one that most people would opt for in the short term. Assessing whether there is "evidence" of malfeasance is a reasonable course.

The challenge for Martha will be that the work climate is already tense, so she may find it difficult to obtain documented "facts" that could be used to report the improprieties. It is also a challenge to determine where she should report the facts, in the event that she actually uncovers evidence.

The last action is theoretically the correct action, but it is fraught with risk. If Martha turns to any of the directors and investors, and they in turn break her confidence as the CFO did, then there is little hope for her to have a career in the organization. On the other hand, if she does report it, and they honor the request, then the truth might be determined by independent actions of the board and/or investors.

All of that said, what would I advise Martha to do? I recommend that she do several things in sequence. She should stay and continue to monitor, because what she has reported thus far is mostly anecdotal and conjecture. It is advisable for her to try to find clear evidence, one way or the other. She should also begin to evaluate alternative job opportunities. If my relationship with the CEO had become noticeably strained, I would want to move on, as it may not be possible to get past what he views as a breach of trust. Remember, if Martha is wrong about her fears, then she has "wrongfully accused" her boss. It is hard to get over that.

Finally, I would hold open the option of going to the board/ investor group. Should she find concrete evidence, or find another job, she should probably attempt to alert those people quickly. My sense of integrity would not allow me to just quit and walk away. I would feel an obligation to alert somebody that there might be a problem. If this were a public company, the securities regulations require that there be a "hot line" to which potential "whistle blowers" can provide their thoughts. I am the Chairman of the Audit Committee of several companies, and in each instance, we have a system to allow people to come forward with these kinds of suspicions.

SECTION III — The Doctor's Rx

Everybody who wants to be a responsible and honorable corporate citizen wants to know, "Just how do I behave with a "Commitment to Integrity?" As you might suspect, that is both a simple question to answer and, at times, can seem to be an impossible challenge to uphold. The simple answer is, "Always do the right thing, no matter how tempting it might be to compromise your sense of right and wrong." But that is so simple as to be almost meaningless when we are faced with the "real world."

Here are some "real world" tips on how to decide what to do:

- It may seem obvious, but when faced with a question of fact, always tell the truth. That means, if somebody asks you to outright lie, do not, not matter what the rationale.
- When faced with a question about a colleague at work, avoid value judgments about their behavior or personality. The best way to avoid a dishonest or "short on integrity answer" about your associates is to simply say, I do not gossip or talk about people. It does not mean you should not have an opinion; it does mean you should keep those kinds of opinions to yourself. The benefit: you do not hurt somebody and you are not forced to say nice things that you don't honestly believe.
- Be candid, not cruel. It is possible to be critical, without hurting a person or an organization. When giving leadership feedback, think how you would react to the same feedback.

- Never knowingly go to work for an organization that has low standards of integrity or ethics. If you discover that weakness, get a new job. Cultures with low standards of integrity and ethics always become hostile to those who choose to live by a higher standard.
- Never tolerate a breach of integrity in your own behavior. It is imperative you set the standard for your staff. The concept of "tone at the top" has no tolerance for the old saw, "Do as I say, not as I do."
- Never tolerate breaches of integrity in your organization. Set a high standard of expectations, and hold those who fail, fully accountable. You may choose to forgive, but you should never ignore misdeeds. Your staff needs to know that you will not tolerate a failure to behave ethically. Punishment may not be appropriate, but clear and unambiguous "corrective action" must be taken.
- Avoid the temptation to compromise on core values, just because it is convenient.

SECTION IV — Ask the Doctor

Taylor: I have a boss I do not trust. He has actually lied to me about a couple of things during the last several weeks. Today he told me that I am getting a new assignment that would eventually be a promotion, but that right now he could not promote me because he did not have the position evaluated for a higher pay level. He said that he had already submitted the job for an upgraded status and that he was certain it would be approved by HR. I know somebody in HR and I actually checked to see if that was the case. She told me that the job had been evaluated a few months ago and that it was not going to be upgraded. What should I do?

The Doctor: There is one simple answer: run, do not walk to another job. By that I mean, you need to get away from your boss, so if possible, I would request a transfer. If that is not an option, start looking for a new employer. Confronting your boss will not solve the problem, and it will make your relationship with him even worse. I hope that you told the HR person about the lie, but if not, you should. Ask that your information be held confidential. Hopefully the integrity of the HR department will keep the confidence, so that you do not end up in the same situation as Martha.

Beverly: My boss fired me today. I was shocked, and it actually made me cry. I know that my boss and I did not get along, so I guess I should have seen it coming, but I did not. Now what do I do? I need a job, so how do I get one when I have been fired? Do I tell prospective employers I was fired? If so, how can I expect to be hired?

The Doctor: I am very sorry about the job loss. It is terribly painful and crying is not an unusual reaction. You have asked a great question, and there is no easy answer. As we all know, seldom do CEOs who have been fired issue a press release that says "I've been fired, please hire me". Typically, the corporate press release reads "Mr. X has resigned to pursue other interests". Most people know this is code for "fired". So, what are your options?

This is a real test of integrity. The correct, highest integrity thing to do is to say "I was fired". Unfortunately, you are correct that such honesty will not play well with potential employers. My advice is that you try to avoid talking about it. If pushed to explain how and why you left your last job, say that the job was not the right fit. The law in the US actually helps because, unless you stole money, or some other terrible thing, previous employers are not likely to say more than that you worked there and the dates of employment.

I have an additional piece of advice. The place where your integrity matters the most is within yourself. You need to honestly assess why you were fired. I know this will not be easy, but I also know that employees are seldom fired because they did not "get along" with their boss. Think about how and where you failed, and then focus on what you can do to prevent that from happening at your next job. If you want you to succeed, you will have to take action to repair your weaknesses. I also suggest that you seek guidance and advice from someone who will be candid with you. Sometimes a third party can help us through these issues and provide insight into our attitudes and behaviors that we might not see on our own.

LEADERS WITH THE BEST-LAID PLANS

LEADERSHIP INVOLVES MAKING PLANS: business plans, strategic plans, action plans, daily task plans, goal and expectation plans. If you are working and achieving according to your plans, your business will very likely grow and require new plans. Plans are not static, and must be reviewed and revised on a regular basis. Sometimes your plans will require just a slight tweak, and other times your plans will need a major adjustment. Regardless of how good you are at planning, the best laid plans are useless without the people and systems that will turn the plans into results.

The activities and plans in my consulting organization are reviewed and revised on a regular basis. During a review several years ago, it was determined that we had the right people in place, but that too much time was spent, and too many opportunities wasted, because we didn't have an effective Client Relationship

Management (CRM) system to support our goals. We researched and tested a variety of CRMs, and concurrently honed our list of "Must Have" capabilities. Our ultimate choice was one of the more expensive options, but we correctly anticipated that the results would outweigh the cost.

The CRM we chose had two distinct advantages: 1. It met our extensive capability requirements which included handling a large database of contacts and emailing this newsletter to thousands of subscribers. 2. The system came with a CRM Sherpa who was dedicated to support, train and help the customer implement all aspects of the system. Having our own designated Sherpa was a critical aspect of our ability to fully understand and utilize all of the CRM's complex functionality. Unfortunately, this is a lesson that we learned the hard way. More than a year prior to this we tried a different CRM that was also complex, but didn't come with a designated support person. We jumped in without any training other than a webinar demo, and as a result made a few big mistakes. The mistakes set us on a path of frustration, and lacking sufficient training or support, we ultimately dumped the system. When implementing a new system, it is critical that at least one person, either internal or external, is fully knowledgeable and able to train the other users.

Everyone in my organization was involved in training for our new CRM. We started by doing tutorials on our own, and then together we attended online training sessions with our Sherpa. At our first group training session, we were more or less equally informed from our individual work with the online tutorials. Our Sherpa gave us a plan of action steps that we should take to reach each subsequent level of training. After the third or fourth group training, the second lesson of "systems" was evident: training is essential, but not all trainees learn alike. My associates and I have varying degrees of comfort and savvy in regards to computer technology, and it does not correlate to any notions about age or sex. Some people grasp technology easily, and others find it as confusing as a foreign language. A few of my associates were truly intimidated by the CRM and would have given up had we not agreed that it was essential for our business. For leaders, it is important to respect your associates' fears about learning new systems, and to provide them with sufficient training and support to overcome their resistance.

In addition to technical fluency, it was apparent that our individual learning curves and areas of focus differ greatly. This knowledge prompted me to revise the plan of how we would approach the CRM training as a group. It made no sense for all of us to take part in each training session after we were comfortable with its general functionality. Instead, I designated two individuals to continue training. One was an internal "Sherpa" who is a computer whiz and served as the expert/trainer/support person after our CRM-Sherpa's implementation phase expired; the other is the internal CRM "administrator" who was responsible for daily data entry and related administrative work. This readjustment allowed the rest of the team to spend their time on the work that they do best, and that most effectively contributes to our bottom line.

Since the time that we first implemented the CRM, the technology and systems we use to support our business have continued to evolve and improve. As a result, we continue to update our systems and now use "Cloud" technology in our organization.

Regardless of how seasoned we are as leaders, we need to continually reevaluate our plans, and the people and systems that support those plans. When plans change, the changes may be met with resistance or fear, and leaders need to provide their associates with enough support to ease them through the transition. The bottom line is that leaders are responsible for the direction of the organization, and the ability for their associates to succeed. This means being open to change, and having the ability to embrace and implement it.

SECTION II: Mini Case — Pam's New Assignment

Pam is the secretary and executive assistant for a lawyer who left his former firm and started a personal practice. She works part time, because her boss, Bruce, travels extensively and requires only limited support for administrative work. In the first year of her employment, Pam was really happy. She enjoyed her assignments, as well as the flexibility of the job, which enabled her to handle the challenges of being a single mother. After a year on the job, Bruce gave her a positive review, as well as a raise, and said that it was time for her to take on some additional assignments. Among the new assignments was to do the bookkeeping.

In the first year, Pam had been responsible for billing clients for expenses, and keeping track of the checks and deposits for those expenses. That was part of the original job description, and she is good at it thanks to her excellent organizational skills. Bookkeeping is a different story. She is really not good with numbers, nor does she enjoy it. Corresponding with clients, making travel arrangements and managing files are her strong suit; numbers are not. Recently, Pam told Bruce that she was spending a lot of additional time trying to keep the books, and that she didn't feel that she was well-suited for that job. He didn't pay much attention to the complaint, and said that her raise should more than compensate her for the extra time.

Pam is now frustrated and unhappy. She really doesn't like doing the accounting, and struggles with it on a daily basis. Furthermore, she resents that this was not part of her original job description and now it seems that she has to do it or find another job. She likes her boss and would prefer to continue working for him, but the toil of bookkeeping is making her miserable at work.

Who is at fault – Pam or Bruce?

Pam's perspective and unhappiness are understandable, but she may be partly to blame. Did she effectively communicate her unhappiness and ineptitude with accounting to her boss? Or was it an off-hand comment when he was busy and not truly focused on her situation? If Pam didn't talk to him at a time that was set aside for them to have a personal meeting, Bruce may have been distracted or have misinterpreted her comments as a request for additional pay. This type of issue needs to be addressed at a meeting that is designated for focused discussion. Pam may also have failed to be assertive in communicating her discontent, for fear of losing her job. The best approach for her would be to set an appointment with her boss, and to make it clear that she wants to discuss her job, roles and responsibilities. At the start of the meeting, she should describe her challenges, but be open to his response and listen to his side. If they are both open-minded, they will find a good solution.

If Bruce is a good leader, he likely believes that Pam is capable of taking on additional work and that it will help her grow as well as support the business. The problem may be that Pam is resistant to change and learning a new skill. However, he needs to support her in the new assignment by providing a software program that will help her with accounting, as well as outside training to get over her fears and feelings of ineptitude. Keeping the books is taking a great deal of time, and training is likely to improve her speed and skill. Good leaders need to be supportive of their associates when they face new challenges, and to assist them in gaining the necessary knowledge and skills to excel in their work. They also need to recognize when the assignment is simply a bad fit. A bad fit won't be improved by any amount of training, and needs to be resolved with an alternate plan.

SECTION III — The Doctor's Rx

Change is inevitable in the life of a business, and leaders are responsible for indentifying when change is needed. Some associates will be pleased and excited by a change, particularly if that change is a promotion. However, even in the case of a promotion, change can be unsettling and cause fear and anxiety. It may elicit different emotions in different individuals. One associate may view a new system as a welcome means of making work easier; another may see it as a confounding nuisance that makes work difficult. I have one associate who continued to use her laptop when it was well past its lifespan simply because she didn't want to deal with installing new systems and adjusting to a new computer. Not until her computer crashed was she eager to make that change.

Like any fear, the fear of change must be overcome. When a leader determines that a change is necessary, it should be clearly communicated that this is not an optional adjustment. At the same time, every effort should be made to ease the transition. What the leader can do to help:

- Provide training. There is no benefit to having associates thrust into something new and then left to figure it out alone. Training is essential.
- Communicate and keep the lines open. If your associates are struggling, you need to know it and offer assistance and solutions.

- Be a mentor and/or provide a go-to person who will be available for support.
- Offer continuing education. Employees who have the capability to grow or be promoted will benefit from learning new skills.

SECTION IV — Ask the Doctor

From Janet: I'm a Regional Sales Manager for a pharmaceutical company, and for the past three years I have reported to George, the Regional Director for my territory. George and I had a great working relationship, and he pretty much left me on my own because I was very good at sales, and exceeded my quota every year.

Recently there was a shake-up in top management, and after a new CEO started George left the company. I was offered his position, and accepted it because the pay increase was substantial and I thought I was right for the job. Unfortunately, the upper management expects me to be on top of my sales managers at all times, and in addition to making sales myself I have to spend hours filling out reports. My style is much more like George's, and I think that if my sales associates are hitting their targets (which I can see in our shared CRM) that I don't need to babysit them. Apparently management doesn't agree and I am beginning to think I made a mistake in taking the promotion. I'm not sure what to do, and I would appreciate your advice.

The Doctor: It is possible that your new role is truly not the right one for you. Many times in my career as a leader and a consultant, I have encountered individuals who were great at their jobs, and after being promoted to a supervisor position were unhappy and unable to adapt. You were happy and successful in your position in sales, without the burden of being a leader. This might suggest that being in the field and interfacing with prospects and clients is where you are most talented and comfortable. Only you can determine if this is true. If so, hopefully your company will be able to reassign you as a District Manager.

Keep in mind that management has adopted new methods, and that if you return to your former position, your relationship with the new Regional Director will be different from that which you had with George. The changes that have taken place within your organization are not optional, and whether you are a salesperson or a sales team manager, the organization has altered its standards. There is no guarantee that if you join a different organization that its standards will be more comfortable for you. I suggest that you make an honest assessment of whether you want to be a leader. Following that, consider your resistance to change and the steps you can take to overcome it. You might be a brilliant leader if you have training and a mentor to offer support.

THE SEVEN ESSENTIAL STEPS TO LEADERSHIP SUCCESS

IN MY BOOK Lead with Love I use a mnemonic to describe the ten essential steps to leadership success. The mnemonic is LEADERSHIP and each of these letters represents an essential step. While I have simplified the elements of leadership into ten words, the essence of my message is that being an effective, peak-performance leader is simple, but not easy.

The responsibility of being an effective leader is much more important than being an effective "manager". Every effective manager leads first, and manages second. In my lexicon, there are two things the "person in charge of an organizational unit" does: the first is to lead the people; the second is to administer the processes that make up the work. I call this administrative activity the mechanics of managing...these are the activities of planning, organizing, controlling, report writing, etc., and of course the implementation of the technical work of the unit. These are critical activities and can never be ignored, but in my experience those managers who focus the preponderance of their time on the mechanics, ultimately do not succeed. They may achieve short term results, but they usually fail over time.

That which is done "to and for" the people makes a leader a long-term success, not what he or she does to administer the mechanics. Indeed, a manager with great leadership skills can sometimes be successful without being an effective administrator. I have worked for leaders like that, and they were great achievers.

On the other hand, I have worked for leaders who were great administrators but poor leaders, and they were ultimately failures. Simply put: administration may be a necessary condition, but it is not a sufficient condition, for success; whereas, leadership may be a necessary and sufficient condition for success.

My core premise is that if you are to be a successful leader, your success will be determined not by how great an administrator you are, but how great a leader you are day-in-and-day-out. When the staff you are "in charge of" believes that you are a great leader, and when you are doing the ten essential steps, you will be a peak-performance leader who tastes the joy of success.

SECTION II: Mini Case — Do it MY way

Albert was preoccupied and filled with a sense of unease as he drove to the office. He knew that he was going to have another tough day at work. As the Supervisor of Accounts Payable for the last ten years, Albert was confident that he knew how to do his job, and how to do it right. He could not understand how his new boss, Barbara, who had only been there for one week, could have such a dramatically different view of his job.

Barbara had been preaching to Albert about leading his staff, and about implementing new procedures that, frankly, made no sense to him. Having seen hundreds of people churn through the Accounts Payable Department over the years, he had learned from experience that his job boiled down to one key responsibility: getting the transactions paid on schedule, but not a day earlier than required. He personally processed nearly half of the payments in any given day, while the other three staff members handled the rest. If they got the job done, great…if not…they would be gone quickly.

Paying the vendors was not complicated; therefore, Albert did not see a need to waste time on much more than a quick training of new employees. By focusing on productivity, he had a great record of getting the work out, and had been praised for years on the quality of his unit's work. In short, he had a great performance record and couldn't imagine why Barbara was complaining. All her talk about management stuff was just a distraction, and had no practical value in Albert's eyes. After all, he has been supervisor for ten years, and has always delivered what was asked of him. How could someone say *after just one week* that he is not doing his job?

As Albert walked in the door of his office building, his anxiety grew. He had barely settled into his desk chair when his boss came in and started the discussion…

Question: Does Albert have the problem, or does Barbara?

Actually they both have a problem…but our limited knowledge, of the situation prevents us from determining blame in this case. However, we <u>can</u> identify the signs and symptoms of each participant's problems. Barbara obviously thinks that Albert should do some things differently (or do things that he currently doesn't do at all), but she seems to be in an unreasonable hurry to conclude that Albert is not a good leader. We cannot be certain if her concerns are about managerial mechanics such as reporting, quality control, attendance records, etc., or if her problems are with his leadership activities. In either case, she is certainly being very aggressive, very early.

It is easy to sympathize with Albert's puzzlement about her conclusions after just a week of being in charge. Barbara is probably moving too fast, and has not given herself sufficient time to assess both the performance of the work unit and the performance of the leader. Perhaps her predecessor or her current boss has expressed some dissatisfaction with Albert's performance; nevertheless, she seems to be acting in a highly critical manner very early in the relationship.

We would probably advise her to slow down, listen and observe for a few weeks, and then begin to share her informed judgments with Albert. Her problems with him may be right on target, but she probably needs more time to get to know him and his style in order to determine if he is really falling short of the leadership that she wants.

Albert's own problems are evident in his attitude towards his staff and his job. He clearly is not very interested in helping people succeed, and his singular focus on output may mean that he has huge turnover in his staff. In addition, his thoughts about production suggest that he is doing 50% of his team's output, with three people doing the other 50%. Either he is spectacularly productive, or they are spectacularly unproductive. In either case, this discrepancy in productivity poses a real challenge for Barbara.

Albert's thoughts also indicate that he is not very interested in what we would call either the administrative or the leadership work. He is highly concerned with the bottom line, but his role in leading the staff is a low priority. In the long run, Albert's methods as a "doer" rather than a "leader" could be a serious problem. Our only certainty is that this working relationship is strained after just one week, and unless there is a change of course on both parties, it is in serious trouble. Barbara's own boss will most likely have to take an active role in resolving this situation.

SECTION III — The Doctor's Rx
Being sensitive…

When you take on a new job, you should not immediately adopt the notions and biases of the previous boss; it is wiser to make your own conclusions in the first several weeks by doing more listening and watching than speech making. Certainly you need to give some guidance as to your expectations, but you should also be sensitive to the fact that you have now become a "disruptive force" in the lives of your new staff. The change to working for someone new is unsettling and often dramatic. It will take time for them to get to know you…and you to know them. Moving too fast can disorient them, and prevent you from fairly assessing each individual. On the other hand, do not wait for months to pass before making your thoughts known or taking necessary actions. This transition phase is a balancing act, and you need to make certain that the unit's performance is not damaged by one extreme or the other.

SECTION IV — Ask the Doctor
Robin: I have a boss who seems to think I'm so good that I don't need any time for the learning process. She keeps piling on projects that are completely new to me, and I feel like she expects me to have them finished the next day. I enjoy the work but I'm totally overloaded, and if it continues like this I won't be able to meet her expectations. How can I tell her to back off?

The Doctor: The good news is that you are probably right, and your boss thinks you're great. The bad news is that you really have to be cautious in asking her to back off, because you could damage your ability to be seen as a "star." My first thought is to say, keep trying to keep up. Perhaps you are being tested and for now you do not want to cry wolf. Let it go for a couple more weeks, and put in the extra time it takes to get the assignments done, and I might add, done well. The onslaught of new projects may be followed by a quieter period that will allow you and your learning curve to reach a more comfortable balance with the workload.

If the pace does not slow down after a couple of weeks, or worse, if it gets even more demanding, then you will need to talk to her about the problem. Each one of us must decide how much work we can do, and how many extra hours we are willing to put in. If you have hit your limit, and are now passing it, then it is time to have a candid discussion with your boss. The trick will be how you handle the conversation. You do not want your boss to see you as a "whiner", but you need to get your message across. Tell her that you want to do an excellent job, but you simply are running out of time to do a great job. Express your concerns in terms of the quality of the work, rather than the quantity. There is no guarantee that she will react exactly as you want, but if you do not address the issue, you will eventually fail or "burn out".

Jeff: I just started in a new job as a supervisor, and I am already lost. My boss hasn't done anything to help me get started, and the staff is not helping me at all. I have been at this job for about a month now, and I am really worried that I am not getting the job done. What should I do?

The Doctor: It is important to recognize that if you are worried about your performance, then there is a pretty good chance that your boss is as well. However, your concern is not a bad thing, as it is a warning that you need to take action. I suggest you do a couple of things: 1) Talk to the former supervisor, if he/she is still around and find out what you can from them. This may not be just your problem. 2) If you have a good friend in management close by, talk to that friend and see if just sharing will get you some insight. 3) Talk to your boss. I know that sounds like a really hard thing to do, but you must do it sooner rather than later. I suggest that you ask to see your boss, and in that session <u>ask</u> (not tell) him to advise you on how you are doing and how you might improve. My guess is that if you are concerned, so is he, and this will give him a chance to talk to you about those concerns. You need to have this conversation "yesterday" because the longer you go without the feedback, the more convinced he may become that you cannot do the job.

On the other hand, you may be surprised. Perhaps he thinks that you are doing a great job and you are simply being too hard on yourself. A more likely scenario is that he has not yet noticed the situation, so when you talk to him you will be alerting him to your concerns. With any luck, you will start to get some help. If he thinks that there is a problem with the staff, he may think it is your fault, or he may realize that you inherited some staff problems that need to be addressed. In short, there is much more downside in not talking with your boss.

DAY 23

EVALUATION

"LEADERS SUCCEED BY Making Judgments"

When most of us begin our first job, we have been through the process of being schooled and tested for the skills and knowledge that we have gained. Virtually our entire lives, beginning with the first day of school, we have been evaluated on our success. We have been in constant competition, whether it was against the standards for an A, or against an opponent on the sport field. People made judgments about our performances in school, and when we entered the work place it started all over again.

There is no escaping the process of evaluation. Students get grades; workers get performance evaluations. As a leader, you are required to make those evaluations. I suspect that when you gave your first performance evaluation, you realized that all those people who had been evaluating you probably experienced the same emotion you were feeling...anxiety. Yes, every time I do a performance evaluation I feel anxious, even uncomfortable. It is no fun being put in a position where I am the "judge" of someone's performance. I imagine that evaluating your staff makes you uncomfortable as well, even if you're like me and have done it many times over the years.

So why is that? Well, for one, it means that you must have criteria against which to assess the performance (you may recall that these criteria are part of "Expectations"—the first E in LEADERSHIP). This poses a problem for the many leaders who never clearly defined and communicated the expectations. How can you make this evaluative judgment if you, and worse still your associates, are not clear on what the expectations were for the period of evaluation?

Even if you had stated the expectations, how do you make a judgment about how well they were met if you do not have effective measurements of performance, let alone a clear evidence of that performance? On top of all that, most of us know that if we give a positive comment, it may not be strong enough to elicit a favorable reaction from the associate; conversely, if we give a negative or unsatisfactory comment, we can almost certainly predict that there will be a disagreement from the associate. In any case, the conversation can end up being an emotional and maybe even confrontational event. Few of us enjoy that type of interaction.

Despite the difficulties, every one of us has done a performance review and somehow gotten through it. Whether the review was effective is a different issue. Far too many performance reviews are so weak on either facts or focus, that they fail in their intended use as a constructive part of the development process. They become either poor report cards, or perhaps even super high grades, which reflect only our unwillingness to deal with conflict. More often than not, evaluations are done once a year and reflect not our judgments about performance and how it can be improved, but rather our judgments and conclusions about performance and how it reflected success or failure. Indeed, performance evaluations done infrequently are simply too little too late.

Every leader must learn that an evaluation should be made frequently enough to be judgmental <u>and</u> developmental. As leaders we are required to make judgments, but those judgments should start as a developmental effort, not a final judgment and disposition. Yes, we will ultimately need to decide success or failure, but along the way, we must give adequate feedback so that our associates can learn from the critiques. If we do not give that feedback early and often, we are failing our associates. Quite frankly, many people in the work world do not really understand how well they are doing in their jobs, and it is our responsibility to make certain that they do.

If you have done a good job of defining expectations, then the criteria for assessment and evaluation are already established and it is quite simple to tally up the achievement and score the performance. That is the simple part; the "not easy" part is actually giving the feedback. Most leaders, and I am no exception, do not find these feedback sessions easy. Unless you have a super star working for you, there is always something that you will say that will be a negative comment. If your experience is like mine, you know that will engender some disagreement from the associate, and most of us do not like the emotional stress of a disagreement. Nevertheless, that conversation is essential for the organization, you and the associate if you are going to improve the performance of your unit. It is not easy to follow through, but we must make these judgments if we are to assure success in our units.

SECTION II: Mini Case — A "Call" out of the Blue

Jackie has been the supervisor of the call center team for just over a year and it is now time for her to give her staff their annual reviews. Three of her weakest-performing associates are up for review and she is truly dreading those sessions. In each case, she is convinced that the employee is not going to make it, but she is just as convinced that not a single one of these employees will agree with her assessment. In fact, they apparently think they are doing a great job, as she heard from another supervisor that each one of the weak-performers is expecting a big raise.

Since the first of the year, Jackie has been keeping elaborate notes about what each person has done, good and bad. There is no doubt in her mind that she has the facts to support her evaluation of each employee. Once the performance appraisals are completed, she can send the documentation to the HR department, and she is certain that they will be very comfortable with the facts and will terminate the employees. In spite of being confident in her assessment, Jackie is nervous and uncomfortable with the prospect of doing these appraisals. Her boss agreed to her request that he sit in with her, and this afternoon they will do the three sessions together.

Question: What should Jackie do?

Quite simply, I think Jackie and her boss should cancel the review sessions and instead have a meeting themselves. Unless we do not know something about the last year, the story suggests that Jackie has never talked to the employees about their performances. If this is the case, then I suspect that if she goes forward with the performance evaluation sessions as planned, these three associates will come "unglued." There is no doubt that if I were working for a full year and believed that I was doing a great job, only to learn at the end of that year that I had failed, I would be more than a little upset. Worse still, Jackie seems to think that she will be able to take these "facts" to the HR department and that they will terminate the employees.

In my experience, most well-managed organizations have a policy that requires a process of feedback about weak or failed performance because it gives employees an opportunity to improve performance over time. I suspect that Jackie's organization is no exception; hence, it is likely that the HR department would tell her that they cannot support the termination of these employees.

Jackie may not like the idea, but she probably needs to begin the progressive feedback process with these meetings. She should treat these reviews as the first in a series of meetings that will be required to either improve performance or to "build a case" for termination. Any other course of action could be illegal, and at a minimum, would be unfair to the associates.

SECTION III — The Doctor's Rx

Deciding when and where to have an evaluation session is worth a few moments of reflection. The key to this decision begins with the assumption that you want the session to be at a time and place that is conducive to the associate accepting your feedback as valid and constructive. This means that you want the associate to be open to your comments, not resistant. Consider these factors:

- Is this associate a morning person or an afternoon person? Schedule the session when he or she is most likely to be alert and responsive.
- Reviews tend to make even the great performers feel insecure, so choose a setting that is comfortable for your employees.
- Hold the session in a place where you are not using your "power of authority." If you have an office, don't sit behind the desk. If you don't have an office, try a conference room with a round table.
- Reflect on the associate's most recent positive performance, and start out the session with a strong comment about

that success. This is particularly important if you are going to be giving a lot of negative feedback.

- You should dress in an outfit that does not emphasize your power, but rather is more comfortable. Take into consideration your associates' attire as well, and whether they might feel more at ease on a casual attire day.
- Try to avoid sessions when you know that the associate is having problems in his/her personal life. That distraction will make it hard for them to be effective listeners.

SECTION IV — Ask The Doctor

Barbara: I just interviewed the best candidate I have ever talked to, but she wants twice the salary I can offer, what should I do?

The Doctor: That is a great question. My first response is: I hope it was not the first interview, as I always try to avoid salary talks in the first interview. Further, why was this a surprise to you or to her? Did your job posting, advertisement, or recruiter clearly communicate the salary range?

Regardless, you need to be very straight, very early. If we assume you are not the owner of the business, and that there is some HR person or business manager who is setting the salary, then you have a range that is not going to materially change. The candidate needs to know that the salary range is firmly set, and that you will not be able to pay more. Perhaps this will cause the person to walk away, so you must be certain that the range is indeed firm and non-negotiable. If the range cannot be adjusted higher, then you are going to be looking for another candidate.

You should be aware that many people go into interviews with grand ideas. Candidates sometimes ask for the moon and hope that they can compromise on a level that is well in excess of what the employer originally wanted to pay. It is reasonable to assume that your candidate is not firm on the salary that she told you she wants. There is no doubt in my mind that candor on this matter is generally the best policy. You may find that this candidate is "playing a negotiating strategy" and you just need to level with her and say that there are limits to what you can do.

Tony: I interviewed a candidate two days ago, and told him I was going to make a job offer. Now I have found a better candidate. How do I get out of this soup?

The Doctor: It is a bad idea to commit to an offer in an interview, but you know that now. The best advice I can give you is…just tell the truth…you have chosen another candidate. It will embarrass you, and your organization, but you want to hire the best person for the job. Assuming that you have not made the first candidate a job offer in writing, you have no obligation to make a formal offer.

Your predicament is a good example of the reason for companies—large and small—to use a written offer letter as a matter of policy. That way you will be able to say that until you have written an offer letter, there is no job offer.

Week 4

LOVE

LOVE -YOUR FRIENDS, YOUR EMPLOYEES?

HOW MANY TIMES HAVE you heard aspiring managers say, "I want to be in management because I like people?" The simple truth is, someone who does not "like people" is better suited to being a recluse than to being a leader of others. On the other hand, I believe that *liking* people can also be a major impediment to being an effective leader.

I suspect that many of you are now questioning my logic, so let me make it even worse. I believe that it is just great for you to like your dearest friends, but you must not *like* your staff, you must *love* them. I have not chosen the word "love" to be inflammatory. I truly mean *love*, not like. The difference between what *I mean*, and what *you may be thinking* is the key.

When I say love, obviously I do not mean erotic love. Nor do I mean the kinds of love that you have for your spouse or significant other; nor do I mean what you feel for your family members. Indeed, those kinds of love are (generally) unconditional.

Some of you know that "Aloha" in Hawaiian means Hello; some know it means Goodbye; however, it actually means neither of those, it really means Love. The Hawaiian culture uses the word "Aloha" to mean a type of love that we can have--and I believe should have--for all of humanity. This Aloha is the love we feel for other humans because they are uniquely human and that they are the most important beings on the planet. This love of people as humans is what I want you to have for your staff. You should love your staff so much that you care for them simply because they are humans and you want the best for them. On a societal level, that may mean the joy of liberty, equality, justice and the pursuit of happiness. In your organization, it should mean that you want them to achieve excellence in their jobs so that your unit achieves peak performance. What is good for their success will also be good for the unit's success.

As a leader, do not *like* your staff. That may seem radical, but it is an essential element of your ability to lead. Liking a staff member may cause you to ignore mistakes made; and by disliking a staff member, you may ignore the things that are done well. Liking or disliking can cause bias in your thinking, and as leaders we must always remain focused on helping our associates to leverage their strengths and improve their weaknesses. If we cannot eliminate bias, we cannot accomplish that critical goal.

SECTION II: Mini Case — The Friendly Boss

Janet had never been happier in her job than she was two months ago, when she was promoted to Litigation Group Leader in the Miami office of her law firm. Having been part of the litigation group in the same law firm since graduating from law school ten years ago, Janet was proud to be awarded this new responsibility.

It had surprised Janet that the firm's senior partners had chosen her to replace the retiring litigation group leader, as there were several more senior attorneys in the group. Nonetheless, Janet's performance over the years, beginning with working for the most senior litigator in the firm, to most recently winning a really big product liability case for the firm's largest corporate client, had earned her the promotion.

On the day following the official announcement, Janet was proud to receive a congratulations card signed by all five litigation partners in the office. They were all delighted that she had been appointed the new leader because they all considered her a true friend and colleague. That was a major victory for Janet, since the firm had never had such a young partner as a litigation group leader. In short, she had built a warm and comfortable relationship with the other attorneys and it showed in the warmth of their feedback.

That was two months ago. Today was a different matter. Janet was not looking forward to going into work this morning. The firm's managing partner has scheduled a meeting with her to discuss the recent problems in the litigation group. In the last two months, one of the partners in the section (who also happened to be Janet's best friend) had lost two big cases that everybody thought were "slam dunks to win." In addition, two of the best and brightest young associate attorneys had left to join a rival firm. She knew that today's meeting was going to be unpleasant at best. Worse still, Janet felt as though her relationships with the partners had deteriorated. They were still good friends, but she was frustrated by the fact that their performances weren't meeting expectations. Although she had not asked them directly, she also had the feeling that they were not responding to her guidance and counsel.

Question: What caused Janet to go from star to goat?

Well once again, we cannot be really certain, but there are some clues:

It is clear that Janet has developed a close, friendly relationship with her fellow attorneys. They all like her and she likes them. In addition, she and her partners believe that those relationships will work to everyone's advantage as Janet takes on her new role as group leader. It is also clear that Janet is an excellent attorney who had proven her skills in the courtroom. It is *not* clear why the litigation group has suffered from problems in the two months since Janet took over as leader. There is either a huge "run of bad luck" or there is a leadership problem. Unfortunately, I think we all suspect that it is a leadership problem. My guess is that Janet has made the "liking" mistake.

Leading in a partnership environment is not "slam dunk" easy. Many partnership leaders have been challenged by the "I am your partner, not your subordinate" comment from their colleagues. This factor can pose a real challenge, which seems to be the case for Janet. Indeed, the fact that she has not "asked them directly" about the problems indicates that she is a bit intimidated or uncomfortable with being in a position of authority over her colleagues, many of whom are older than she, and all of whom she considers friends.

The most probable reason for the litigation group's recent problems is that Janet *likes* her associates too much, but she has not yet learned how to *love* them. She needs to take her leadership role as seriously as she does her "lawyer" role. She needs to forget that her colleagues are also her friends, and from this point forward, love them enough to have that difficult conversation that addresses her concerns about their performance. Loving them includes dealing with their weaknesses and mistakes. If Janet fails to embrace her leadership responsibilities, her colleagues will continue to see her as a friend rather than a leader. The role of "first among equals" is a challenge that can only be handled if you love your associates, and show it, by being the leader.

In regards to the young associates who quit, their departure may indicate that Janet has a staff problem. She needs to find out their reasons for leaving. It is possible that they really could not learn from the partners, or that Janet's leadership was too weak for them to grow and achieve success. She needs to love the associates enough to make certain that they get the guidance and development they need to become effective lawyers.

SECTION III — The Doctor's Rx

If you are promoted to a Leadership capacity, what should you do to start the job? This is a simple question, but there are no simple answers, as it really does depend on the circumstances under which you are appointed. However, there are a few thoughts that you should keep in mind each time you take a new job:

1. **Interview each person in the group** - Even if you already know everyone, take the time to establish a relationship with each member that says, "You are important to me and the unit, and I want to take the time to focus on only you." This also gives them a chance to tell you what is on their minds. You may be surprised by what you hear.

2. **Stop and Listen** – Take your time, even if you have been there for years and think you know what needs to be done. It's worthwhile to take a figurative step back to look at the unit's activities from your new perspective. Taking the time to observe and listen will pay huge dividends in not only what you do, but how well you do.

3. **Take clear, decisive and thoughtful action** – Do not wait too long to take actions; and when you do, the first decisions you make should be ones that you are highly

confident are correct and will be accepted well by the team. This will send a clear signal to them that you can make sound decisions and will avoid having them second-guess you from the start.

4. **Remember what your job is** – For most of you as a Manager or supervisor, you are still a worker, but with the added responsibility of a leader. Do not let the team think that by being a leader you are going to slack off in your contribution, but at the same time, make certain that you show them that you know that you are now the leader and that they can look to you for that being something new you will do. Remember, you are leading people and that means you need to focus on them more than the work.

SECTION IV — Ask The Doctor

Kim: I was just appointed project manager of an information technology project in the IT department of a large corporation and two days into the job, I have discovered that my best friend in the group is holding up the entire project. I have known him for ten years, and worked side by side with him for the last five years. I cannot bring myself to tell him he is a problem, what can I do?

The Doctor: Well Kim, I have a simple question for you… Do you want to stay in your job as project leader? If you do, then you must get over this "I cannot talk to him" mindset. You either need to talk to him, or you need to resign from the project leader position…I am afraid those are your only two options. Now, I am assuming that your assessment he is holding back the entire project is accurate. If so, then you have an obligation to love all of the other associates on the team, and to love your long-time friend enough, to face the facts and to deal with it. His failure is hurting the other associates on the team, hurting him and hurting you and your attempt to achieve the mission of the team. Liking your friend is getting in the way of loving him. You need to think through tonight the discussion you will have, and then first thing tomorrow you need to have a conversation with him that clearly, but sensitively, communicates to him his failing.

Bill: Last night at dinner with one of my associates, she asked me to give her two days off. The problem is we are faced with a huge and critical deadline and I really cannot let her go. She pleaded with me and threatened to quit if I did not let her go. What can I do?

The Doctor: I must admit, my first reaction would be…Ok, quit! Now I know that's not what you wanted to hear, and it is probably not what I would say, but your associate cannot be allowed to threaten you. You need to sit back down with her and tell her that you would be happy to consider the days off at a later time, but unless it is an emergency, you just can't let her go right now. In addition, you need to tell her that if she does not understand the sense of urgency, you would be happy to explain it again. As a closing comment, I think it is essential that you tell her that threats are not an effective way to maintain or build a quality relationship.

By the way…I hope that having dinner with her had something to do with work, otherwise, you need to be certain that you are not building a "like" relationship that might get in the way of being a quality Leader.

Robert: I have been with my current employer for four months. During that time I have worked to be part of the HR team that is in place and to learn the culture of the organization. There are two women in the Department that for lack of a better word, dislike me. I have talked to my boss about the issue and I have addressed the issue with the two women. With 20 very successful years in HR, this is the first time I've met people that acted like they don't want to work with me. What steps should I take to open better communications and to establish trust?

The Doctor: I cannot tell what the hierarchical relationship is with the two women, but I suspect that they are more like peers than superiors or subordinates. Assuming that is correct, and knowing that you've had four months to assess the situation, I sympathize with your problem. I also suspect that this HR Department is not a huge one, hence your ability to remain in your current position will require you to resolve the problem.

All of that said, my first advice is to recognize that there is a pretty good chance these folks have worked together for some time and your presence upsets that comfortable balance they have had. It is also possible that you are seen as a threat to their jobs. I suspect that with all your experience, they think that you may become a career blockage for them, or even become their boss.

My suggestion is a great deal easier to make than to take: give it more time. These folks may be intentionally trying to make your life miserable, but you are the newcomer and you need to demonstrate, not through your words, but through your actions and performance that you want to be a productive member of the team and that your goal is to be helpful. A simple idea may be to look for a moment when one or both of them appear to need some help and extend yourself to help them, and make certain that they know that you are doing nothing to take credit for that help. My message is, you need to bite your tongue and try to get them to find it to be a good thing that you are there. Keep trying and most likely they will get the message that you are not a threat to them and that you really are a nice guy.

25

AGAPE VS. EROS

MANY OF YOU, UPON reading the title "Agape vs. Eros," will immediately know the subject that I am going to address in this Issue. If you are not familiar with these terms, then I hope that you will get a copy of my book <u>Lead with Love,</u> and read about the topic in greater detail. This is not a raw marketing ploy; it is a sincere effort to inform you about a critical issue which has been in the news lately and which we, as leaders, must cope with every day.

I begin my book with the rather provocative assertion that "Friends Like but Leaders Love." The premise is that to be effective leaders, we must have a deep caring for people that transcends *liking* our staff and certainly avoids friendship. Indeed, if we *like* or *dislike* our staff, we run the risk of developing strong, potentially hurtful, biases toward our staff. In liking someone, there is an inherent positive bias that may cause us to ignore weaknesses and exaggerate strengths; in disliking someone, we may exaggerate weaknesses and ignore strengths. Only when we "love" our associates do we have the ability to be truly objective and effective in their development and ultimate success.

There are a variety of Greek definitions of Love; Eros and Agape represent two critical definitions of Love which are particularly relevant today. Eros is the root of erotic, and represents the kinds of love that are at the core of most human sexual relationships. We can dismiss this type of love, as clearly it is the wrong definition in relation to leadership. Agape is best described as the feeling we have for human beings, just because they are humans and creatures of God. This love transcends all personal relationships and focuses on the class of beings we call humans. In essence, we love all people, irrespective of their personal characteristics and behaviors. The corollary to this concept of love is that we should help our fellow humans to live a good life.

We cannot be effective leaders if we do not know how to love, Agape style. When we can care about our associates, simply because they are humans, we can then care so much about them that we can act always with their best interests at heart. That means that the individual and group interests are the primary focus of our behavior. We will lead them to success, and we will do that which is in the best interest of the organization and sensitive to the best interests of the associates.

Several years ago, a headline story illustrated what can go wrong when Agape is not leading the way. In this particular instance, the CEO of Boeing was forced to resign because of an apparent extramarital affair with a subordinate female executive in the company. Obviously, this situation generated a great deal of commentary from a variety of analysts and "talking heads," most of whom I believe were missing the critical point.

All too many people, from Wall Street to Main Street, essentially gave the CEO a "free pass" on this issue. Their views were summed up in the comments, "The board should keep its nose out of the bedroom" or "This was a great CEO who did nothing worse than what a former President did, and that President was given a pass by the Congress." Several well-respected writers and commentators simply accepted the CEO's behavior as a private matter, without questioning the consequences of this behavior in respect to his role as leader. They argued that this matter did not rise to a level of significance that the company should have lost a great CEO who had been instrumental in dramatically improving the company. They also cited evidence that the company stock fell on the announcement, confirming that "Wall Street" and the investing community was not happy with the decision.

I firmly believe that the Boeing Board of Directors took the correct action, and I am appalled that there were serious observers who sought to diminish the importance of this breach of trust by the CEO. My concern about these reactions has nothing to do with the moral or ethical considerations of an extramarital affair and their impact on the corporation. I am also not judging whether this action was a violation of the code of ethics, as I have not reviewed their documents. My position is entirely based on an appraisal of the CEO's judgment, and the impact of his actions in light of his role as leader of the organization.

Quite emphatically, there is no place in the workplace for bad judgment by the leader. This CEO's bad judgment added even more damage to an already weakened corporate reputation. Leading up to this event, Boeing had been embarrassed by a variety of serious executive missteps and illegal acts. For the CEO to act in a way that would (if discovered) harm the company's image was horrible judgment and could easily have been adequate cause for sanctions by the board.

But, that is not the real poison in this CEO's misdeed. This CEO damaged his ability to lead the organization by compromising his ability to love all of his associates (Agape) by loving (Eros) one of his associates. It is impossible to imagine a plausible defense that the CEO could have given if faced with the criticism that he had a biased view of the subordinate's behavior and performance.

A CEO cannot be personally involved with a subordinate and have a wholly professional view of that subordinate. It is unrealistic in this case to think that the CEO had an objective view of his lover's job performance. Further, it is clear that there was no way for the affair to have been so well hidden that other associates in the organization would not be impacted by the relationship. Clearly, all associates who knew of the affair would believe that the CEO "favored" the sexual partner, and any actions that resulted in a positive reference to that partner would be suspect. To think otherwise would be naïve. Lastly, there is no way that the sexual partner could ever really believe that the CEO was indifferent to her performance. In short, the CEO was biased in favor of the partner and all in the company would have accurately concluded that a lack of objectivity existed.

This extramarital affair is an extreme case of *liking* your subordinates. Intensifying the *liking* to the level of an erotic relationship simply magnifies the internal, psychological conflict that the leader experiences. The temptation to favor the lover will be almost irresistible and will eventually taint the objectivity so essential to assure fairness to all associates.

The added risk of business judgment being influenced by the partner is not insignificant and must be viewed as a cancer to that same objectivity, let alone the potential of compromising corporate security. I suspect that some board members in the Boeing case were also concerned about how the participants in the affair might react in the event that an associate decided to attempt to blackmail the couple in order to preserve confidentiality.

In short, you cannot expect to have an affair with a subordinate, extra marital or not, without a negative impact on your objectivity as a boss and your judgment as a leader and key decision maker. The risks of the relationship are clear and far too high for a leader with good judgment to ignore. It is indeed a tragedy because it is clear that the Boeing CEO had achieved much, but those achievements would have begun to diminish as the leader lost the ability to be objective. Although I would agree that the ethical considerations are not irrelevant, the failure in leadership judgment by this CEO was so serious that I believe the Board of Directors had no other course of action. Because organizations committed to sound leadership would have no choice but to follow the same course of action with you, I caution you to never allow yourself to like an associate so much that you fall into this erotic trap.

SECTION II: Mini Case — John and Marianne

John has been a hard-working, top-performing accountant in the Accounts Payable section of his organization for over six years. During the last year he has been dating Marianne, who is an accountant in the same department. The two have fallen in love and are starting to think and talk about making a permanent relationship. They have been very discreet about their dating and to the best of their knowledge, nobody in the section has any idea that they have been dating.

Last week John was promoted to Supervisor of Accounts Payable, and he has been asked to review the staffing in his section to see if there is a way to reduce staff by one accountant. John has already done that review and has concluded that it would be possible to make one cut by combining two jobs and eliminating some redundant processing controls. He plans to recommend to his boss that Marianne's and Joan's jobs be combined, and that Joan, as the weaker of the two, be either transferred or terminated.

Questions: Was there any problem with the relationship between John and Marianne? Is there now? Does John have a need to disclose his relationship with Marianne? What should John do about the analysis of the staffing in his unit? What should Marianne do? What should the company do?

Thoughts: In today's competitive work environment, many employees are putting in long hours and sacrificing free time. As a result, the workplace is one of the best opportunities for forging personal relationships, and meeting potential mates. John and Marianne have had no reason to be embarrassed about seeing each other, and their decision to keep the relationship quiet may or may not have been a good idea. However, John's promotion has significantly altered and complicated the situation.

John is now Marianne's boss, and the two of them have a real challenge. John should have had discussed the conflict with his boss on the same day that he was appointed supervisor. Now, it is not just a good idea, it is a critical action. John simply cannot allow himself to remain Marianne's boss, and he needs to deal with that immediately. The situation is complicated even further by the staff analysis, and worse still, his conclusion and potential recommendation.

In one short week John has gone from having a great, smooth sailing career, to facing a potential crisis if he does not act quickly and correctly. Where this will end up is dependent on John and the action that he takes. He must first tell Marianne that he cannot continue as her boss; following that he must have a candid discussion with his own boss. Then John and his boss need to deal with the staffing question. The easiest solution would be to move Marianne out of the unit, but that may not be the best thing for the company or for Marianne. We do not know enough about the facts of the situation, but what we do know is that there is no way that John's boss can allow John to make a recommendation to move Joan out and keep Marianne.

This situation must be handled both carefully and quickly. If the company is large enough and there is the opportunity to have either John or Marianne move to another unit, that would be great assuming that the new assignment works for the company and, the individuals. If the company is small with no alternative career options for either, there could be no easy answer to the dilemma, short of one of the two leaving the company.

The John and Marianne scenario is fairly common, and companies and supervisors have a tendency to ignore the problem. Nothing could be worse. These kinds of situations do not just strain the relationship of the individuals, they strain the company and all it's associates. It is now necessary for John and Marianne to make certain that the associates in the section are aware of the relationship. It will not make the matter any easier, or make the problem go away, but it will make it possible for all associates to know the truth and deal accordingly until the company and John conclude what they will do.

SECTION III — The Doctor's Rx

What if you find yourself in a situation where you are dating a colleague who gets promoted to a position that is two or more levels above you? What can you do to avoid any problems? The best tip I can offer you is to either get out of the personal relationship, or get out of the reporting relationship. Also, if it is not generally know that you are dating, make certain that it becomes public knowledge so that, at the very least, you will not be accused of having a clandestine relationship. You may not need to move immediately, but I think that it will be in your best interests to avoid the potential conflict.

Despite the challenges, I do not believe that it is necessary to categorically rule out dating anyone at the office. After all, it is likely that you share common interests with your coworkers, and one of them could be just the right person for you. I do suggest, however, that you not try to hide it. Once it is known, then you can be certain that, should a promotion be considered, that fact will be understood. It may not seem fair, but as you could see from the case above, should one of you get promoted, it will be awkward to solve the problem.

SECTION IV — Ask the Doctor

Bernice: I have a brother who works for me in my section. Do you think that this is a problem?

The Doctor: The simple answer is, yes probably. However, there are notable exceptions, such as in family businesses where relatives of the owners work for relatives in the company and do so successfully. Many corporations have nepotism rules that prohibit such situations, but in family businesses these rules seldom exist.

Having a relative work for you runs all of the same risks that I outlined in the previous scenarios involving personal relationships. In my personal experience, I have owned a business where my daughter worked for me; even now, she is a consultant to one of my companies. I love her very much and we have a great father-daughter relationship (or at least I believe we do) but the business relationship interjected into that personal relationship always has its challenges. I can't deny that I am positively biased in favor of my daughter, and I am not capable of being entirely objective. It is a real test for me. My daughter, on the other hand, has always been very good about keeping the roles separate...in fact she does a much better job than I do.

It is impossible to be completely objective with a relative, but if your relative is a star, and everybody believes that you work hard to be fair in your evaluations of that relative, then it would be folly to change it. The real problem can develop if your brother's performance fails to meet your standards, and you are incapable of holding him accountable for the required performance. If you do that, it will not be long before every associate in the section or company will know that you are biased, meaning that you have compromised your credibility as a leader

DAY 26

CARING

IF YOU'VE BEEN READING this book one day at a time as prescribed, you know by now that the effective use of the word love in the context of leadership is very special to me. Last week while I was working with a client, this concept was being met with some resistance. It occurred to me that such resistance is not only predictable, it is actually very common. Indeed, there was a time when this word, and the core concept, was simply not a part of management vocabulary. There is still the tendency, particularly in the male dominated leadership society, to avoid using words like "love" because they convey softness.

After thinking more about this, I started a conversation with a very good friend who happens to be a graduate of one of the military's officer training programs. He told me that looking back on his early days of "being in charge," he actually started his managing career as a first class "SOB." He told me that the first time he was really in charge of something, including people, was not in his first real job after graduation, it was when he was in that program.

He has been in the civilian world as a very successful leader for many years, yet he believes that his experience in the training program was one of the most valuable in relation to becoming a leader. Obviously, this program is designed to be one of those places where the future leaders of the military start their journey to the top, and he was fortunate enough to have been pretty successful in the first two thirds of the course. In fact, as a senior, he had managed to become the highest ranking student in the program.

As the last year unfolded, he took his responsibilities very seriously. His peers considered him to be intense and highly-focused on being the best student in the program. Even he recognized that he was stern and tough, leaving little room for compromise and setting very high standards for his fellow students. In short, he was well on his way to finishing first in his class, a ranking that would be determined by a combination of academic scores and leadership evaluations by the officer staff.

When it came time for graduation and the final rankings, he was not number one. He was number two and he was devastated. After being ranked #1 throughout virtually the entire time in program, and not having done anything which varied from the past, he was puzzled to say the least. The only explanation he could surmise was that the leadership evaluations had changed and therefore he had been scored lower in the final rankings than previously. There was nothing he could do except graduate as number two, but the experience left a huge hole in his pride.

As a result of his excellence in the academics, he was assigned to teach at a school at his active duty station. Ironically, that assignment made him a fellow instructor with one of the same officers who had been his evaluator.

As you might suspect, he got to know the other instructor on a personal level, and then eventually asked the big question. This answer stunned him…he said, "You were great at every level, and several of us talked about you any number of times as being one of the best we had ever seen, but, we also saw a part of you that simply fell short of a great leader, and eventually that caused several of us to mark you down on leadership."

Well, that report did not make him feel any better, so as you can imagine, he pursued the next question to find out what it was they did not like. It was then he learned that, even in the tough and disciplined military, leaders who did not know how to show "love" to their peers or subordinates simply could not be effective. This officer cited several examples where my friend had ordered disciplinary action on a fellow student (one nobody really liked) where that person had clearly violated a core rule. They criticized him because it was clear to them that he appeared to "enjoy the action." These officers were convinced that he was not doing it to accomplish "tough love" but rather to just be tough. In short… he did not "love" the person he was punishing.

My friend told me he was stunned, and it took him a long time to assimilate that learning into his behavior, but he was being forced to get inside his own head and to decide what kind of a leader he would be, one who thought of the goals only, or one who thought of both the goals and the people. Fortunately, he eventually had a mentor a few years later that helped him find the balance.

I personally can identify with this story, because during my early days as a leader, I did not focus on how to carry out tough actions in a loving way. As time went on, I saw boss after boss make the same mistakes I made as a young leader. They liked some staff members and disliked others. They were biased in favor of their favorites and clearly biased against their least favorite. Like my friend, I too had a mentor who helped me learn my lesson. I hope that all of you who are reading this book have somebody who can help you make the transition into a loving leader.

SECTION II: Mini Case — Joe and Kelly

Joe is the supervisor of the second shift in housekeeping at a very upscale hotel in a resort area. He had worked there for over three years and had begun as an entry level employee at that time. He had worked hard and had consistently been rated as Outstanding in every performance appraisal he ever had. He is an intense worker and has been working very hard to have his shift be the highest rated group in the hotel. He has some very high quality staff and has been able to gain a great deal of recognition for his group and lots of people in the hotel have expressed an interest in joining his team.

His intense focus on success and growth is driven by the fact that he is engaged to be married and he wants very much to buy a new house. He has not told anybody at work about his impending marriage because he does not want people to know that his fiancé works in the accounting department and they have decided to keep their relationship secret until the last minute. The company has a strict policy about spouses working in the company, so one of them will need to get a new job, and she is likely to be the one to leave. They are afraid that if they let people know now, she will need to start looking immediately because her boss is not very sympathetic.

On the other hand, Joe has several people who recently have left him and joined another hotel down the street. He dismissed these departures as normal, but clearly they put a dent into his plans. Kelly, one of his favorite staff members has been with him about three months and he just really enjoys having her on the team. She has made a few mistakes, but he likes her so much that he has overlooked them where he might not have with another employee. In fact, yesterday he watched as she and another staff member got into a bit of an argument which he stayed out of because he did not want to intervene, mostly because he thought that Kelly was wrong and he did not want to embarrass her. In short, Joe covered for Kelly on this one, and it was not the first time he did that.

Today, Joe was called into his boss's office and was told that there were serious rumors flying around the office that Joe and Kelly were having an affair and Joe was given a formal, written warning that the company would not tolerate such behavior.

Question: How did this happen to Joe and what should he do?

Joe is trapped in an absurd situation where the allegations are not correct, but the problem is generally one of his own making. Joe has been covering so much for Kelly that everybody who works for him has come to the conclusion that he must be having an affair with her. Otherwise his actions make no sense.

This may seem like a ridiculous example, but it actually happened to a fellow supervisor a number of years ago. His only way out was to quit and start over. Unfortunately, he never really changed his behavior and he ended up being fired from his next job because he simply could not focus on performance instead of personality.

SECTION III — The Doctor's Rx

Here is a tip that many leaders have a tough time being committed to: Do not make friends with associates who work for you! Now, this advice is predicated on a couple of assumptions: 1) You like being the boss; 2) You know the difference between like and love.

You must be friendly, but not a friend. Do not make the mistake of becoming the friend of your staff, because eventually they will need to be treated as somebody who works for you, not your friend. Avoid socializing with them, avoid getting involved in their personal lives and avoid enjoying them as an individual. Do act in a friendly manner, be caring about them and their families and do show them that no matter how you relate to them, that you will always be fair, objective and focused on their results at work. In short, care about them, care for them, and be caring about them as workers; hence, love them.

SECTION IV — Ask the Doctor

Mary: My boss told a friend-of-a-friend of mine that he cannot stand me. What should I do?

The Doctor: Well, if that is the truth then I have only one question…Does it show?

I know that may seem trite, but it is critical. As we have said many times, the like or dislike thing can be very damaging either way, but if you actually have a quality, professional working relationship and you believe that he is being fair, then you do not have a problem. If the answer is that it does not show in any way, then you may be able to live with the situation.

I do have some concern that he would tell somebody how he feels about you, so you should be careful. This a yellow flag about him. To tell anybody that he has a problem with you is unprofessional, so there is a real need for caution here. You should watch carefully and make certain that you monitor his behavior, and indeed, watch your own. Since you now have this added insight, it is going to be tough for you to hide the fact that you have heard such a thing about yourself.

One last thought: I would make certain that you no longer talk to your friend about his/her friend and the connection to your boss. This set of relationships needs to be kept out of all this process. In addition, the minute you sense that the attitude is impacting the behavior, then you should address the issue by either talking with your boss about it, or…make a decision to get away from this person. Recognize that as much as I advise leaders not to let the like/dislike bias get in the way, as a subordinate, you need to try to avoid working for somebody who dislikes you, or who you dislike. Eventually these emotions, if strong enough, will shine through and get in the way of the relationship.

John: I am not a supervisor or leader, I am one of those workers you talk about. Here is my problem, I am a research chemist in a lab and I have fallen for my boss. She is fantastic and I am convinced that we would be a great couple. She is so caring that I just sense that she actually feels the same way about me. At the same time, I'm aware of the general caution against pursuing a romance at work. What should I do?

The Doctor: Well, this is not the first time this kind of a situation has developed. My advice, get a transfer. Nobody would benefit from your having a non-work relationship with her, and frankly, you may actually be wrong about how she feels. How does she act with the rest of the staff? If she is a truly loving person, then every person in your lab will have the sense that she is sensitive and caring toward them as well. It is entirely possible that all you are seeing is her ability to love in the Agape sense, as opposed to the sense that you seem to want to believe in.

Whatever you do, do not mix work and sex. It is much easier to do that, when you no longer work together. If she really is interested in you, then after you no longer work for her, you can find out if she will date you.

27

DO YOU LOVE
YOUR JOB?

FOR THOSE OF YOU who have read one of my books or who know something about me, you realize by now, that I get great joy in being involved in a great many of "things," and I love that! My board memberships are many and diverse; my business consulting clients are different enough to be fun and anything but boring; my corporate board clients are from a wide range of industries and the governance, leadership and strategy work I do is intellectually challenging; the companies I am invested in provide me with a continuing involvement in managing operating businesses; and all my writing keeps me focused on growing and learning. In short, all of that adds up to a pretty exciting and full professional life. I am seldom in need of something to keep me busy.

A few years ago my concept of "busy" changed when I decided to commit to one of my consulting clients that I would become a part of the management team. I was truly excited about helping this company become a world class player in its niche, and decided that I could do that, while not abandoning any of the other activities I am engaged in. I have some very capable staff in support of my business engagements, so I was quite confident that I could handle the added work load.

Just as I was getting started with the new commitment I got hit by another major challenge, which my wife describes as the "straw that broke the camel's back," (or if it did not break the back, it bent it very significantly). For years, my wife has told me that I really do not know how to say "No." Actually, I have never disagreed with her, but I also always managed to survive the "over-extension" and actually came out at the end of the day, pleased with my contribution. I have also been blessed with a wife, and life partner, of over 40 years who must love me enough to know that working at things that matter is what makes me who I am.

What was the event? Well… that is "the rest of the story." As you may know, I am on the board of directors of Junior Achievement Worldwide, a non-profit organization that is truly global in its reach. I have been involved in Junior Achievement (JA) since I was a student as a youth, and I have served on the Board for many years which enabled me to have a very broad range of involvement in a variety of roles. I have great passion for the organization and what we do "To inspire and prepare young people to succeed in a global economy." Each year we change the lives of close to 8 million children all over the world by helping them to learn about the world of entrepreneurship, business and the economy which all ends up giving them life tools, not just knowledge of the free enterprise system.

As part of the Executive Committee of JA, I was present when the President and CEO announced that he was resigning to take a job in the medical services field where he had worked prior to coming to us about six years before. From a board perspective, there are many lessons to be learned from this event, but the plain fact is, as a board we did not have an answer to the succession challenge this left us with. There was no consensus choice from within the organization, and consequently we concluded we needed to do a formal search that would look at both internal and external candidates. Well, with that decision, we still did not have a solution to what we could do to lead the organization while the search was on. We had several retired CEO/Executive board members who I thought were very obvious candidates to step forward and fill the interim role as CEO. Unfortunately, each of them said that they would be glad to help, but none was willing to take the job for what would probably be about 6-9 months. We were stuck.

Yes, you guessed it…Once again I could not say, NO! The Chair of the board managed to talk me into being the President & CEO during the interim period. So, at the height of this extremely "busy" time, I took on my third "full time job."

I was working harder and longer hours than ever, and considering the crisis management experiences I have had that is a mouthful; however, I was having the time of my life! My commitments and activities were vastly different, yet they all had one thing in common: I was leading very competent and committed associates towards exciting goals.

To this day, I have the same excitement for my role as a leader. I am in a position to help people win, and the irony is, I am so overwhelmed with things to pay attention to, that there is no way that I can ever really micro manage these associates, so they are getting leadership that is empowering, not leadership that is confining. I love my job(s), and I hope you love yours as well, because there is nothing more energizing that wanting to go to work so that you can feel good about the time you spent. Indeed, if you love your job, it is not work, it is the joy of fulfillment. When that is the case, the job(s) will never tire you, they will never burn you out, because you will take more energy from the job than you put in.

SECTION II: Mini Case — Caroline's Empty Nest

Caroline has been in her job for 25 years, and has always been evaluated as a solid performer in that job. She has seen five bosses, come and go, and has continued to do the same job with the same, high quality results. She has five children, and a husband who travels long distances almost 80% of the normal work week, so she has been very much alone much of the time she has been working. The fact that she has been able to continue to do the same job has helped her because she was unable to do much more than go to work, do her job, and then at 5 PM every day, go home to be with the kids.

About a year ago, Caroline realized that, as an empty nester, she had a good deal more time on her hands. She had been getting home at 5:30 every night, but now, the kids are not there, and neither is her husband. All of a sudden, Caroline was bored. Worse, that feeling of boredom has started to spread to her feelings about work. The once comfortable, no stress job that she could probably do "in her sleep," has started to "put her to sleep."

About six months ago, Caroline talked to her boss and asked if she could be considered for a move to another job, maybe even a promotion. Her boss, David, responded with, "Caroline, why would you want another job, you are doing an excellent job where you are and I really cannot imagine anybody doing a better job." Caroline had never really asked for a new job, so when she got that answer, she just accepted it and went back to work.

During the last six months, David started to see deterioration in Caroline's performance. David actually had several instances where Caroline made rather serious errors and he had to have a couple of tough counseling sessions with Caroline about how her work was slipping. She responded that she was sorry, but each of the incidents was getting more serious and last week, David had another very difficult session with Caroline. He told her that her performance was unacceptable and that he was putting her on probation.

Caroline did not take that session well and went home that night early without telling David she was leaving early. The next day David told Caroline that he wanted to know why she left early and she said that she was so upset about the discussion they had that she needed to get away. He was furious and told her that he could not tolerate that kind of behavior and that he was going to talk to HR about her and recommend that she be transferred because he could no longer rely on her.

What should David do?

Well, I am afraid that David should take a deep breath and start asking himself how a twenty year, excellent performer, could go from that to unsatisfactory in the same job, during a six month period of time. If he asks that question, then I would hope that he would take stock of the first conversation Caroline had with him six months ago. His blatant disregard for her request was the first mistake he made. The second was to not ask why after all those years, Caroline wanted a new job. In fact, the real question probably should have been, how could Caroline have been happy working in the same job for twenty years. If he had asked those questions, he would have realized that there were factors in her life that made the job, basically a very distant second priority. Her children came first during those years, so she was "content" to stay doing the same thing. Once they were out of the house, she was all alone and needed something else to fill the gap. She wanted the job to be more substantial and actually asked for it, but did not know how to insist upon it. Slowly, the boredom set in and she started making mistakes.

David, as the leader needs to focus on the fact that behavior does not change overnight. All behavior is caused, and if Caroline's performance is deteriorating, there must be a reason. Unfortunately, the real reason is David's failure to respond to her request or listen to and probe further. David may be able to save the day if he stops right now and goes back to talk to Caroline about the issue, but if he does not, he may have just lost an excellent, long term employee who might have been even more valuable as she expanded her interest in working "for a purpose."

SECTION III — The Doctor's Rx

When was the last time you had a new job? I have had many new jobs in my career as a leader, and it is the most recent set of new jobs that has reminded me that there are many things that a new boss should consider doing in order to get off to a good start. Here are a few of those tips, and I will try to give several more over the coming months:

1. This may sound silly, but have a meeting. Yes, as quickly as possible, get your new group of direct reports together in one place and have a meeting. This is not a "transactional meeting" but rather a meeting where you get the team together to just connect them with you. You can use it to lay out some thoughts you have about your new responsibilities. You can also use it to tell them something about yourself, while each of them tells you a little about themselves. You can also have each of them talk about their experiences in and out of the current organization. The important thing is that they have a few moments to hear from you and that they know that you want to

connect with them. All too many times leaders of a group of direct reports, whether they are clerks or managers, never take the time to tell the staff how they are going to lead. This meeting will give you a chance to tell them something about how you plan to do your job.

2. Another meeting, only this time, one-on-one meetings with each direct report. I think that it is essential that you take the time to get to know each of the people you are responsible for. This meeting can be much more personal and it can also start the process of getting to know them as individuals.

3. A quick follow up to these introductory meetings should be what I call a "deep dive" on the details of the responsibilities you have inherited. Once again, it is irrelevant how low or high in the organization you are, it is essential that you learn, quickly, what it is that your staff does, how they do it, and how you will know how well it is being done. This step is essential and must be done early. Staff can "forgive" a boss for not knowing what is going on in the organization on the first day; they will not forgive you if you do not know at the end of six months. Your staff expects "technical competence" from you and if you fail to learn they will have a very difficult time developing respect of you. There is an even more fundamental reason for you to learn…your boss will expect it. If you do not become competent in the technical aspects of your job, you will never be able to satisfy your boss that you are truly "in-charge."

SECTION IV — Ask the Doctor

Adrian: There is a new boss coming to our department tomorrow, and I am delighted. My previous boss was a jerk, and I am so happy to be rid of him. I have worked in the department for three years and my previous boss never once said a nice thing to me, and passed me over for promotion twice, in favor of a younger and less experienced employee. My question is, how do I make certain that this does not happen to me again?

The Doctor: Well, Adrian, that is a very difficult question to answer. Not because I do not have some tips for dealing with a new boss, but rather because I cannot be certain what the problem was with your previous boss. The comments in your question are just short enough that I cannot decide why your previous boss was a "jerk." If I assume that you are doing an excellent job, then it sounds like you had a very weak boss. If I assume, on the other hand, that you are not performing well, then you might have had a weak boss who did an inadequate job of communicating your weaknesses; or you might be ignoring all of the feedback he has given you and could be in "denial" about your performance.

One thing I do know is that you need to answer those questions, very honestly. If you really are not doing the job effectively, then the best advice I can give you is, improve. If you have had a weak boss, then you can look forward to at least a chance to build a new relationship.

That said, no matter what the case, if your previous boss did not think you were doing a good job, your new boss will probably hear that from the previous boss, and will be influenced by that observation. Hopefully, the new boss will give you a chance, but you are probably going to have an uphill battle. I suggest that you enter the new relationship with the new boss recognizing that and making certain that you do not show an "attitude" with your new boss. For certain, avoid "bad mouthing" the previous boss. That will only set you up for your new boss thinking you have an attitude problem.

I do have one piece of added advice. Many years ago, early in my career, I had a person work for me who did a remarkable job of convincing me that he was on my team. We had worked together as associates in the same department, but when I took over the responsibilities for that department, he almost immediately became my most trusted staff member.

After several years of working together, I remarked one night when we were cleaning up a particularly troublesome problem, that I really appreciated his commitment and loyalty, and I told him that I had always been amazed at how quickly he became so important to me. That was when he told me that his father had given him some advice when he first entered the workforce, and that advice was probably key to his behavior. He said, "My father told me that as soon as I had a new boss I should find out what he liked or wanted, and then give him/her more of it than anybody else."

It struck me that his father was a very wise man, not because he was a "suck up" but that he realized that the boss is the boss, and that the best way to get accolades is to achieve the results that the boss wants/needs. In the long run, that is what makes organizations work.

28

REWARDS

"AN ORGANIZATION ELICITS the Behavior It Rewards"

When did you first learn the word "No?" You may not remember, but I suspect that you learned it from your parents, and you were probably pretty young as well. In fact, it was probably so early, that most of us have no recollection of the when, but certainly we remember the meaning. This negative word carries great power since many of us learn what "not to do" much earlier than we learn what "to do." Frequently, we also got the message that our parents were unhappy with us, and the result of that was some type of rejection or even punishment. Another kind of negative learning, for example when we touched something that was hot, occurred when we experienced pain along with the "No." It did not take long for us to learn to stay away from the hot object.

Unfortunately, negative learning tends to continue through much of the rest of our lives. Too much of what we learn is the "what not to do" and we find out "what we should do" by trial and error. We get lucky when something produces a positive result, so we try it again. Enough times and we find a success pattern that we can follow.

Returning to the infant example...when we discovered that by using our arms and legs correctly we could crawl to another location, we perfected that process. Our curiosity was satisfied and we learned a motor skill. When we crawled to our parents, or later walked, we got stroked by them and their praise, excitement, loving touch or even a reward of a cookie or a sweet, gave us a learning that was powerful and fun. We probably then did it over and over again and before long, we would be walking and eventually talking.

Ironically, some of our "other than No" learning is also the result of making a fuss and getting what we want. As infants, we could not speak, so we used our bodies and our screams to let our parents know that we were hungry, tired, uncomfortable, or even in pain. Each time we screamed, we got our parents' attention, and they usually solved our problems. It does not take long for babies to learn that lesson that when they are hungry they should simply cry and then they will be fed. This lesson is reinforced for many years, and as the child gets older there is a good chance that the lesson of the hunger cry will be applied in the form of a temper tantrum thrown by a child not getting its way. If the parents, in order to stop the tantrum, respond with exactly what the child wants, the child learns to associate that behavior with success. The "No" learning is replaced by the yes learning. The message is that throwing a tantrum will result in getting what you want.

This visit back to infancy truly does have a great deal of relevance to our work as leaders. The key lesson is that we can learn from the "NO" response and even punishment, but the best learning occurs when we are rewarded for success. When our associates do something wrong, we can easily criticize them, or even punish them with negative feedback. This will obviously get the point across, but may not get them effectively trained. We are teaching them "what not to do" not the "should do" or "to do." Punishment puts the focus on what you do not want, but praise highlights what you *do* want. In short, rewards can elicit the behavior you want.

But just like the parents with a baby, we can also inadvertently reward behavior we do not want. When we allow staff to violate rules and not suffer the consequences, we are essentially telling them that the rules aren't important and it is ok to break them. If you fail to stop, counsel against or punish inappropriate behavior, it is the same as rewarding it. Reward that behavior and you will get more of it.

Great leaders discover that the most powerful learning takes place when we reward the behavior we want. As leaders we all must remind ourselves of this truth and act on it. The old expression, "catch your staff doing something right" is incredibly powerful. The message is clear: decide what you want, look for it, then reinforce the behavior with rewards that tell your associates what "to do" rather than saying what "not to do."

SECTION II: Mini Case — Late Again

One morning about three months ago, Bill turned off his alarm without being awake and alert enough to realize that it was time to get up for work. He had been up until 3 a.m. preparing for an exam in his marketing course and he simply needed more sleep. By the time he woke up, it was 8:30 which was exactly the time he was due at work. To make matters worse, he was scheduled for a meeting at 9 with his boss.

Bill made record time getting ready, and by 9 AM he was in his car driving to the office. He got there at 9:20 and ran from his car to the conference room where the meeting was scheduled. The room was empty, which made Bill even more concerned. By the time he got to his boss's office, he was practically frantic with worry. "Ted, I am so sorry. I was up until 3 AM working on preparation for my mid-term in Marketing and this morning I turned off the alarm without realizing it."

Much to Bill's surprise, Ted was not upset and said. "I understand Bill, and we cancelled the meeting and decided to reschedule it when you were here. What time would work for you?" Bill was floored. He told Ted the best time for him and they scheduled the meeting for the afternoon.

After they rescheduled, Ted asked Bill to stay for another minute and proceeded to tell him that he had gone to school for his MBA ten years ago, and that his own experience with studying late and oversleeping made him sympathetic to Bill's situation. He even went so far as to tell Bill that he would handle some aspects of Bill's job if he had a problem in the morning again.

This morning, Bill slept in again because he had just finished an "all-nighter" studying for a statistics course. Bill was not concerned, since he knew that Ted had allowed him to be late many times over the last several months. He felt fortunate to have Ted as a boss as it was making his work on the MBA much easier.

By the time Bill arrived in the office, he remembered that he had been expected in a meeting that had been scheduled for 7:30 this morning. Ted had made a point of reminding everybody last night, but Bill was so tired that it had completely slipped his mind. He went straight to the conference room, but the meeting was over. Ted was in his office and as soon as Bill walked in, he saw that Ted's boss, the Vice President of Sales, was there as well. Ted started the conversation with, "Bill, this being late in the morning and missing meetings has become such a serious pattern with you. The meeting this morning was to announce that my boss is leaving and that I will be taking over as the VP of sales. We were planning to announce that you and Jane would be considered for my job, but your absence made that problematic. After the meeting, we gave some more thought to the situation and I am sorry to tell you that we have decided that Jane is our "candidate."

Question: Who made the mistake?

Well, that is actually not an easy question because both Ted and Bill were wrong. The sad fact is that Bill has a bad work habit that got even worse primarily because Ted failed to make clear what "not to do." Ted sent a strong signal to Bill that is was Ok not to come to work on time. That probably was well off the mark because all Ted tried to say was, I am understanding and reasonable. Unfortunately, Bill learned from that first time, that Ted was flexible. As Bill developed the pattern with subsequent tardy behavior, Ted compounded the problem by not addressing the issue with Bill.

In the final analysis, the real cause of the problem is Ted. The leader is responsible for ensuring that the associates know what is expected of them. Ted not only failed to make the expectations clear, he actually rewarded Bill for being late by accepting his tardiness the first time and then by subsequently failing to reprimand Bill when he was late again. By the time of the latest incident, Ted shows that he has ignored the failures by being willing to consider Bill for promotion.

As leaders, we must be careful that we not only make clear what the expectations are, but also that we reward the right behavior. In this case, Ted probably failed on both points and the real loser was Bill.

SECTION III — The Doctor's Rx

You are probably familiar with this point, but it's a critical tip nonetheless: monetary rewards work, but praise often works better. Most of us like to be recognized, and even the most self-assured associates need to be rewarded for their positive behavior and results. Take advantage of every opportunity to acknowledge a good performance. If a staff member does something right, tell them so. If they do something truly great, then make a big deal out of the results.

On the other hand, do not reward associates out of proportion to the level of success. If all they do is to achieve the minimum that is expected, then acknowledge the achievement, but do not establish a reward that communicates delight on your part. (The exception might be when prior failures were so significant, that the success, no matter how small, is actually a break through.) If you have set a high bar for expectations, then make certain that you do not send a signal that low performance is great. If you do that, you will get low performance and your staff will never strive for the high bar. Remember, you will get the behavior you reward, so please make certain you reward what you want, not just what you get.

SECTION IV — Ask the Doctor

Pete: I have a staff member, John, who has worked for me for three years and who has gotten an exceptional performance review each year and a salary increase to match. I just heard through the "internal grapevine" that he is quite unhappy in his current position and has been looking for another job. I must admit, I am shocked. His salary reviews have been far beyond what any other staff member has gotten. How can he possibly be unhappy?

The Doctor: Pete, you have just made the mistake of thinking that a great salary increase is the only reward that matters. It does matter if you fail to get the increase, but the increase itself is not very effective in communicating your belief that this person is a star. The performance appraisal should have sent a strong signal. Since it seems not to have done that, either you did not discuss it with him or the appraisal was not viewed as a real positive reinforcement of behavior and results. If either is the case, then you lost the opportunity to positively communicate with your staff member, and you need to take action immediately to correct that.

On the other hand, you may actually have another problem that could be even more significant. In most cases, when associates are unhappy in their jobs, they frequently are unhappy with their boss or something their boss has done or not done. I have no idea what your relationship is with John, but if there is any chance that you are falling short as a leader, then that may be the entire problem. There is no easy way to deal with this type of situation, but as you will come to understand over time, I believe that direct dialogue with the other person is usually the best approach.

I suggest that you have a chat with John and try to find out what is bothering him. I would just level with him and say, "John, I have heard that you are not completely happy in your job. My source is not important, but I really think you are doing a great job and I want to know what I can do to make you feel more comfortable. Are you willing to share with me, or to give me some thoughts on how I can make this job meet your expectations?" You may not get a straight answer, but it is in my mind worth a try. My experience is that when you openly ask people to help, they will respond by trying to be helpful.

29

"FROM LOVE TO SELF"

REPRINTED FROM THE BOOK *You're In Charge... What Now?*

Our journey began with understanding the role of love in setting the tone of the relationship with your associates and concluded with a focus on creating a positive self-concept and being a leader to yourself. Between committing to honing your capacity to love associates and the role of loving and leading yourself you must set expectations, make a correct assignment, focus on development, provide effective evaluation, and deliver timely rewards. These leadership practices are necessary to foster, encourage, and assure peak performance from your associates. However, the real intensity of your efforts must be on yourself.

The role of leader places a burden on you that cannot be treated lightly. When you were an individual performer, your capacity to deliver results was the true measure of your success. As a work leader, you will probably continue to do tasks that generate results for your organization, but your true measure of success shifts dramatically. You must help your associates achieve success as individuals and as a team. You must not allow the term Work Leaders to confuse you. You are not leading the work; you are leading the workers.

Your role is entirely new since now you must get your greatest happiness from the success of others rather than from your own. This is not a selfless act. It is quite self-focused. As a Work Leader, your only avenue to success is for your unit to succeed. Having a staff to lead means that the organization believes more than one associate is required to achieve the unit goals; hence you alone cannot achieve success. Your staff's pain of failure or excitement at success must be yours. Your goal must be to help staff members stay focused on the goals, because their achievements will be your achievement.

The most effective way for your associates to grow and succeed is to learn from you. Once you are the Work Leader, you are the guiding light. You must be a bright beacon guiding them to achieve. Unfortunately, most of us are not ready for that role and responsibility. Few of us ask for it. Being the appointed leader usually comes to us because we were good at doing the work, not because we were groomed to lead.

We have focused on the key principles required of an effective Work Leader. We have tried to emphasize the simplicity of the concepts, but the actual tasks of leading are tough work. Just as you needed to be trained to do your previous work assignment as an individual performer, so must you be given the boost required to develop the skills of a leader. There are few shortcuts to this development, and although most organizations recognize the challenge, few have discovered the secret of developing peak performance work leaders. All too often, as in our example earlier in the book, work leaders are "thrown into the water" to sink or swim with no real swimming lessons. Most Work

Leaders tend to "doggy paddle" their way to survival, but many never learn to swim. They simply learn to avoid drowning. Are you one of those?

Just as in the case of a child, the only rational way to learn how to swim is to be taught by a person who has the knowledge and skills. The best way to learn how to lead is to work for a great leader, but if you are one who has been left to "sink or swim," we recommend you take action immediately. Find a great work leader, and then find a way to get into that unit. The payback will be enormous. Armed with the seven key Work Leaders principles, you will have the knowledge to develop the skills and attitudes you will need to learn to swim.

You need to become the great Work Leader that all associates want to work for. When that happens, you will have made the transition from Worker to Work Leader.

Just as importantly, once you have gained the skills required to be a great work leader, then it will be your turn to pass on your knowledge, skills, and attitudes to your associates. The reason is simple: somebody in your unit will probably some day be asked to step into your shoes as work leader. One of those associates is probably working for you because he or she wants to learn from a great work leader. Because you love them all, you owe it to all your associates to help your successor be more ready than you were.

SECTION II: The Rest Of The Journey...
If you have enjoyed the insights from this book, then you can also benefit greatly from reading my books, *You're In Charge... What Now?* and *Lead with Love.* Those books are designed to help leaders at every level to be better at leading the people they are responsible to and for. They are loaded with practical insights, just like we have tried to do here. Not "rocket science"

just practical thoughts, many of which you have already heard and seen before, but when brought to your attention, might just change you as a leader.

SECTION III

"Managers are a dime a dozen, but leaders are priceless. Teaching principles as solid as setting expectations, and as radical as understanding love, Gerald M. Czarnecki's seven steps put the new leader's focus where it belongs--on finding, developing, and rewarding teams of outstanding performers. Any manager aspiring to leadership would be wise to study Gerald's advice."

—**Jeff Taylor,** Founder and Chairman, Monster.com

"Recently appointed to your first position leading others? This book is for you! It describes in concrete detail exactly what it takes to get those actually doing the work of the organization to perform at exceptional levels. Powerful, accurate and, most importantly, eminently useable, Czarnecki's insights provide a concrete blueprint for managerial success." Jerry I. Porras, Lane Professor of Organizational Behavior and Change, Emeritus, Graduate School of Business, Stanford University and Co-author of Built to Last

"*You're in Charge...*" is outstanding reading for first time managers as they strive to expand their leadership capacity. Gerry Czarnecki distilled his years of experience at all levels of an organization into an easy-to-read, pragmatic primer on making the transition from supervisor to leader."

—**Edward B. Rust Jr.,** Chairman & CEO,
State Farm Insurance Companies

"If you are a working leader, and you want to get things done, this book is for you. This book is full of practical insights and tips to make you a more effective leader." ~ **Ram Charan**, Consultant to CEOs and Board of Directors and Co-author of Execution

"I loved this book. The concept of "work leaders" is the most compelling and effective approach to blending the role of managers and leaders. It is a practical, comprehensive approach that can truly help "work leaders" be successful in every organization."

—**Rhoda Olsen**, President &
Chief Operating Officer, Great Clips, Inc.

"You're in Charge...What Now? is a perfect textbook for a "rookie manager." The seven essential steps for Work Leaders Success are nicely organized to facilitate the learning process. Each Chapter has Tips to guide the learner, and each chapter ends in a case study with thought provoking questions. I could easily see this book being used to augment management training – with weekly reading assignments followed by group discussion."

—**Gary Davis**, Executive Vice President, Chief Human
Resources and Administration Officer,
J.C. Penney Company, Inc.

SECTION IV

While this book is an expression of my personal thoughts and advice on becoming a better leader, I do not work alone in providing resources, support and guidance to leaders on all levels. I am also the President and CEO of The Deltennium Group ,an alliance of speakers, trainers, coaches and consultants with diverse professional backgrounds and areas of expertise that make us uniquely capable to assist all variety of leaders and organizations. We are committed to engaging, energizing, training, and facilitating the development of organizational and individual excellence through effective strategy and leadership.

Deltennium offers a range of programs that can be used to train everyone from first-level sales managers to top-level boards of directors. Every individual and organization faces unique challenges, and Deltennium works accordingly. My associates and I are flexible and adapt our speaking, training, coaching and consulting engagements to meet the needs of the individual or organization. The goal is success, and whether it's the aid of a book, seminar, coach or consultant that you need to achieve it, you'll find that Deltennium can help.

30

LOVE- FRIENDS LIKE BUT LEADERS LOVE

STOP. DO NOT WRITE off this concept. Everything a leader does begins with a capacity and commitment to love. This is the theme and central core of this book, and there is little doubt the use of that word will rankle the typical leader. But you got past the title of the book, so now you are about to find out how this book uses that term, and why it is the key word in the book.

You must understand that I am not a product of the "flower child culture." I am an early baby boomer who never even came close to being part of the drug-using, peace movement. I was not a protester against the war in Vietnam, and indeed, I was on active duty as a US Army captain during the Vietnam War. I went back to graduate school when the war was unpopular, and I attended classes with the students who turned the country's attention from Vietnam, but a "peacenik" I was not.

If you look at any recount of my leadership and managerial history you will find that I do not even have a "soft" reputation. Throughout most of my professional leadership career, I have been a change agent. Some will call that a euphemism for "tough guy who fires people." Indeed, in some ways, that was true. As a change agent, I spent much of my time fixing broken organizations. Many times, that meant terminating personnel. In short, I have legitimately been seen as a firefighter who did what it took to save organizations and jobs.

I make these points about myself because people who have worked closely with me over the years know that the principles in this chapter guide my every action. The principle of love drives my every leadership act, and I hope that you will read this chapter to understand why I believe that any leader, whose objective is to achieve peak performance and results consistently over the long run, must begin with love.

This chapter leads off the series of key principles reflected in the word LEADERSHIP, but this key idea about love ends up in the title for only one reason. Organizations, no matter how technical, no matter how mechanical, no matter how structured, are comprised of people working together to accomplish a mission or a goal. Take the people away and there is no organization; there are ideas, theories, even dreams, but without people there is nothing but infrastructure, not organization.

Since people make up the essence of organizations, people working together in some type of structure are the essence of how goals are achieved. Science, technology, processes, real estate, machines, natural resources—all are brought together by the humans who "band together" to accomplish a task, series of tasks, and ultimately a goal. The economists define the factors of production as land, labor, capital, and entrepreneurship. For our purposes, these factors are all combined into an organization that uses those factors to create results and, for the economist, goods and services that will have value in a market system.

Since people are why these resources are brought together, and since people are the glue and the brain of this organizational entity, we are driven to focus on how those people function, how they work together, and how their pooling of efforts creates value to the society. It is this pooling together, this set of human interactions that makes it possible for organizations to achieve goals. This is not a philosophical treatise; it is a reality. Without people there would be no goals; without people there would be no achievement of the goals.

With that, the role of the leader becomes much clearer. The leader is the one who assembles the people and the various other "factors of production" to achieve the goals or, in our society, to create goods and services. Most economists who added the concept of entrepreneurship to the classic "factors of production" were forced to admit that there needed to be something that organized the factors of land, labor, and capital. We who have led organizations know that the term *leader* is much more reflective of the thing that ties the factors together.

Love is not used in this chapter to be inflammatory or sensational, although there are some who will charge that is my intent. *Love* is not just a word being used to carry a revolutionary message. It is the only word that can define the essence of this book. Once again, love is at the heart of all leadership activity, and it is that core concept that is embedded in every chapter of this book.

Love. In order to delve more deeply into this word, we actually need to look into some history, in particular, Greek and Hawaiian history. Let's start with the Greeks. What does the word *love* mean, especially for us in this context? The idea of love having a place in the workplace may be disorienting, especially if you're thinking of the kind of love the Greeks called "eros," what we know as sexual or erotic love. Obviously, eros is not the appropriate type of love for leaders to practice in the workplace. Indeed, inappropriate sexual relationships with a coworker—or worse, a subordinate—hold the potential for tragedy for all concerned.

The Greeks also used the word *philia*, which defined another type of love—the love that we have for family. When William Penn first settled in the New World, he named his first and most important city Philadelphia, "the city of brotherly love." The Greek word *philia* was at the heart of the name of his new city. He dreamed Philadelphia would be a city where people would treat each other as brothers.

The concept of brotherly love, or love of family, is a warm and sensitive type of love. It avoids the erotic or sexual aspects of eros, but goes well beyond friendship. The Greeks, and much of Western civilization, believe the bond between family members, in general, far exceeds that of any other relationship. Most of us would agree that our relationships with our family members are strong and critical elements of our own personal development.

This type of unconditional love has great emotional and spiritual appeal. Unfortunately, leaders cannot be this emotionally tied to those for whom leadership is their duty. In many ways, the unconditional nature of this type of love can be more damaging than helpful to a leader. Leaders of organizations, such as boards of directors, have a responsibility to be judgmental. Also, they must be focused on an organization's progress toward and achievement of goals and objectives.

Whether you are a non-executive chair of a religious college board, a development committee chair of a non-profit organization, a council member representing your constituents in a city government, or the chair of an audit committee for a huge public corporation, you have a duty to your group, and to your constituents, to achieve goals. As good as unconditional love may feel in any of those settings, any team member who is not pulling in the same direction is a potential risk to the objectives. You must be prepared to focus on achievement, in many cases to the detriment of an obstructing individual. Brotherly love probably will not help you take the actions necessary to persist on the course to goal alignment and achievement. Indeed, if your affection is so strong that it supersedes your duty to the mission of your organization, it may hinder your effectiveness.

So, let's move on to the third Greek word for love, *agape*. This word reflects the notion that we, as members of the human species, have a special duty to love other members of the species. This love for humankind is the form of love that drives activists to support elimination of the death penalty, causes philanthropists to give vast sums to charity, inspires caring people to volunteer in third world countries, and leads people to help those affected by disasters. We all have that altruistic part of us that wants to give to society or at least to others in need.

This is agape, the fine art—and even emotion—of loving people as members of humanity. It means we have a sensitivity to them that exceeds being polite. It means we pay attention to them, beyond just keeping them from being angry with us. It means helping them just because they are people—not necessarily because they are nice people—and helping them even when they find accepting help difficult. It means telling them bad news with sensitivity. It means not being brutally frank and blunt. In short, it means being aware of their needs, feelings, and difficulties. This type of caring is discussed in many ways by many authors. John Maxwell says it very explicitly: "Effective Leaders know that you must have to touch people's hearts before you ask them for a hand. That is the Law of Connection. All great communicators recognize this truth and act on it almost instinctively. You can't move people to action unless you first move them with emotion. The heart comes before the head."[1]

So, now what about the Hawaiians, and how can the residents of that far-off island chain be of any help? Hawaiians have a unique culture, formed by their great reliance on and attachment to the land. After the brutal consolidation of power by a warlord, King Kamehameha, the Hawaiian culture settled in for a long era of peace and relative prosperity. The culture created a sense of community and relied on a deep commitment to extended family. In addition, during that period, a culture that was highly isolated, yet homogeneous, became a culture of warmth and human sensitivity.

This cultural fact was evidenced in many aspects of the language, but no single word reflected that culture more than the word *aloha*. Most modern-day visitors to the islands think of the word *aloha* as a greeting having one of two meanings, hello or goodbye. Indeed, that is the most common use of the word, but it is actually the least meaningful. In the Hawaiian culture, *aloha* has many meanings and many uses, but the true importance of the word rests in its use to mean "love." When a Hawaiian says to you, "Aloha," what is really being said is "I extend my sense and emotion of love to you." If you are arriving, it means "welcome with love"; if you are departing, it means "go with love."

Indeed, those who have visited the islands may remember that the Hawaiian people express the culture as being a manifestation of the "Aloha Spirit." Therein lies the true meaning. *Aloha* means that "I will live in and among my society with my fellow citizens with a spirit of love." This is the true meaning of love for the Hawaiian culture. To live in love is to live at peace with oneself and with nature. It is this commitment to the love of humanity that defines the ancient Hawaiian culture, and it is this spirit of aloha that can define what is meant by love as the first principle of leadership.

I do not want to suggest that the Hawaiian culture is one without conflict and tension. Indeed, in recent years, there has been great tension in the society. But the root of the ancient Hawaiian traditions is "aloha," and the core values of the society demand a respect for humans and for nature. The small island state depends on a quality balance with nature and with the humanity assembled on their isolated islands. We in the rest of the world have much more opportunity to feel disconnected from each other and from nature, but the roots of our existence are embedded in each other and in nature as well.

It is this connection with humans and the desire, even need, to love and be loved as humans that define our uniqueness as a species. We may be the only species that feels this type of deep connection, and that factor makes us need to complete ourselves by beginning all our relationships with a connection that the Hawaiians called "aloha." It is this sense of aloha (love) that must precede our actions as leaders. When we feel that emotion, only then can we take actions that reflect a true concern for the humans over whom we maintain oversight, governance, and dominion. These functions are reliant on our ability to be servants to their needs while at the same time committing our energy to achieve the goals of the organization.

Why Not Like Instead of Love?

You may ask, "Why use the word *love* when the word *like* would be easier? Why not say that every leader must like people?"

For our purpose, the word *love* is more accurate and less confusing than the word *like*. Indeed, the proposition that leaders must like those they lead is flawed. When you like a person, what does that mean? Usually it means that person's personality characteristics, core beliefs, character traits, or even physical appearance, for some reason, appeal to either your emotions or logical thought. The person may have treated you nicely, smiled at you on a day you were unhappy, complimented you when you needed confidence building, or helped you think through a personal or business problem. You may even have an unexplained bond with that person, which made you feel an emotional attraction almost immediately. You may have nothing in common or everything in common, but you feel comfortable being around that person.

In the same way, liking your associates can help you to enjoy the people you lead. It makes you feel good to lead people you like. In turn, since the chemistry usually goes both ways, the people you are leading will probably like you and feel good about you. If all of this good comes out of liking, then what is wrong with the idea that you should like the people you lead?

Here's what's wrong: How many situations have you been in where you could say that you liked everybody in the group you were leading? If you have a group of two people, then you might expect that you will like both of them. However, most of us are charged with the responsibility of leading larger groups. If you are a sales manager who takes over a sales force of ten, the odds of not liking at least one person in that group are much greater.

Let's also hypothesize that the one person you do not like, for whatever reason, is also the top salesperson in the group and has the highest customer loyalty. In addition, that person has the best relationship with the manufacturing division and has always had the highest peer group ratings as well. At this point you might say, "If this person is that good, then obviously I would like her." Indeed, that might be true. The opposite happens frequently as well. You can have a top performer you truly dislike. If you have been a leader for any period of time, you have been in that situation and probably have struggled with the consequences.

If liking is a requirement of good leadership, how can you lead this person? By that definition, you cannot. So what do you do? Your dislike usually becomes a barrier to communication. If you do not like a person, it is very difficult to hide your dislike. The other person will sense how you feel and begin to react negatively to you as well. Slowly, you begin to distance yourselves from each other in an effort to avoid the undesirable contact. Worse still, you will invariably become overly critical of the person. Eventually these tensions will result in either termination or transfer of the subordinate. Bias wins every time.

Like and You May Be Sorry

Just as "philia," or brotherly love, can be damaging for leaders, so too can liking be dangerous. You may decide to be the leader of only those you like so you will not be challenged by conflict. That is often the next step along the destructive road of leading by liking. Since you want to like everybody who works for you, you begin the process by favoring the ones you like. In many cases, you look past the weaknesses of those you like and become highly critical of those you do not like. The process of favorites or "teacher's pets" begins. Even though your intentions may be honest and pure, you begin purging your staff of all those whom you do not like. Before you are finished, you have a team of people you like. It may or may not be a great team, but you like the team members and they like you. Maybe they are all friends as well. This friendship will probably influence your decisions, on occasion to the detriment of the organization. Bias wins again.

What is wrong with these scenarios? You could argue that nothing destroys a team more than a person who just does not fit in. Indeed, that can be very true. One rotten apple can spoil the basket. But what if the rotten apple is one of the people you like? Doesn't that make the problem more complex and sometimes painful? This is especially true if the friend has come to believe that the relationship with you is more important than the leadership relationship. Remember, as a leader your primary mission is to drive peak performance, not build a team of people you enjoy being with. That may make going to work fun, but it may also create serious conflict for you when a friend fails to achieve peak performance. Unfortunately, when this condition exists, leaders have a tendency to ignore the problem until the entire basket is rotten. Again, bias wins.

A more common problem is a leader's inability to see weakness in a liked person. We all have a tendency to overlook, if not ignore, weaknesses in the people we like. Indeed, we have a tendency to inflate their strengths as well. As a result, we may be so completely blinded that we cannot truly be objective about performance. Remember, as leaders we are almost always accountable, either to ourselves or to a higher authority, for results that match the goals or objectives of the organization or unit. If we are blinded by liking, then we will never be able to evaluate the performance of the group or an individual in it. Often this situation causes shortfalls in performance or failure to achieve goals. At that point, most of us will attribute the failure to external factors rather than conclude that we have failed ourselves or that the team or its members have failed. Bias wins again.

Keep that notion of chemistry, or people liking each other, in mind. If a team is formed from a group of people who do not like each other, it is important that they learn to love each other. This sense of caring, in spite of the lack of liking, is crucial to team success. You do not need liking to create warmth; you need love. For this reason, when Allan Cox talks of warmth in *The Making of an Achiever*, we assume he means the kind of caring that comes from loving your associates. "Warmth is catching. It is easy to discern those companies where warmth in management has caught on. From first contact with the headquarters receptionist to the head of custodial services in an outlying plant, a visitor who walks the halls of a warm company and chats with its people senses the team-play and pride that pervade its atmosphere."[2]

LEADERSHIP TIP
Avoid the Liking Trap

- You probably do not like at least one person who works for you today. Make three lists: (1) all the qualities you do not like about that person; (2) all the good qualities of that same person; (3) that person's primary duties and objectives. Now evaluate that person's performance against his or her objectives.

- Pick the one person you like best in your work unit and make the same three lists and do the same performance evaluation.

- Now compare the two sets of lists and evaluations. Answer this question: which person is the better performer, and why?

- There are probably several people who work for you that you like. Are any of them friends of yours? How long have they been friends? Do you socialize with them? How did you get to be the boss of the unit? Did you work in that unit alongside your friends, or did you come from outside the work unit? How do you feel about being your friends' boss? How do they feel about it? What would you change, if anything, about your unit and the staffing? What will you change in how you are managing the unit and the people you like?

- Have you ever fired a friend? Have you ever been fired by a friend? Are you still friends? What did you learn from the experience?

Back to Love

The contrast between "like" and "love" is both striking and critical. You can love (agape) people and not like them. No one is capable of liking everybody in the human species, but we can love (agape) everybody. As a leader, you must be able to care for all the members of your group, whether you like them or not. Only in that way can you give to your associates the commitment of truth, unbiased behavior, and help in achieving their goals.

Effective leaders have a strong ability to communicate their love to the group they are leading. Regardless of the dynamics of the day-to-day behavior of the leader, the group members must perceive they are being loved. Vince Lombardi was, as many great football coaches are, notorious for yelling insults at his players. Yet, in the face of such apparent disrespect, Lombardi was a loved coach who earned affection because players knew he loved them.

Leadership style is not the issue. Style is a description of perceived patterns of behavior, not necessarily a reflection of the internal capacity to love. In some style or personality types, it may take a little longer to determine if the capacity to love is present, but the lack of that capacity is almost always obvious. It seems that you can always detect a mean streak, or a lack of love, much faster than you can identify a real capacity to love.

Don't Fake It

It is almost impossible to hide a lack of love. Somehow those who pretend to have agape seem to give themselves away. "All the world is a stage," Shakespeare said, and many leaders are great actors. Some acting skill is probably helpful because even the most sincerely loving leader sometimes has a bad day. At these times, acting that provides encouragement and enthusiasm can often be a valuable leadership tool for the leader. On the other hand, people in leadership positions who continually pretend to be loving ultimately create trauma for those they lead. It is irrelevant how good the acting is; a leader's actions will speak louder than words or body language. Over time it is almost impossible for a "non-loving" person to hide the lack of human caring and agape.

The Pain of Working without a Loving Boss

Most of us have worked for non-lovers. One boss made me feel uncomfortable just being in his presence. I was his chief financial officer (CFO), and very early on he made it clear that he knew my job better than I did. He never actually had to say anything to cause me to doubt myself. After several months of this unexplained fear, I dreaded going to see him. And the situation was getting worse, not better. Each encounter created another bad experience for me, and probably for him as well.

I had a difficult time understanding what was happening to me until one day when we were discussing another person who had caused some difficulties in the company, and he said to me, "I do not trust him, but then, I do not trust anybody. And you, Gerry, your problem is you trust people. My advice to you is to recognize that the people who work for you are just human resources of the business, and you need to use them as if they are expendable. The only thing that matters is that we get the job done, and that means you need to check up on everything those people do." (As you might expect, I was working for a different company in less than six months.) This boss never understood that love and trust are the foundation of all human relationships. In fact, he never could check up on everybody all the time, and ultimately his subordinates failed him and the company. He never evolved into a leader, and he sank along with the company as it went into tragic decline. In this case, his employees' failure was his.

Agape is a state of the rational mind as much as it is an emotion. Loving others does not guarantee they will love you. Indeed, if you trust people and they do not reciprocate, you will have trouble. That is why some, like my infamous boss, would say you should never trust anyone. It is true that some people whom you love as humans will not repay your trust. Some people in this world are lazy, dishonest, uncaring, unloving, or just plain incompetent. However, no leader can be effective without a deep love for people as human beings.

The spirit of aloha is not always easy to follow. Many times in your career, you will encounter somebody who simply is not "likeable." That is the real test of aloha. It is not our responsibility to like our associates, but it is our responsibility to have aloha for them. When I lived in Hawaii, because so much of the culture was shaped by the "aloha spirit," it was impossible to not have aloha on my mind. Even those of us who were not native Hawaiians were always reminded of the aloha culture, and I know that it influenced how I reacted. Most of us in the workplace do not have that factor "keeping us honest," so we must rely on our commitment to be great leaders.

We leaders need to have love at the heart of everything we do because we are responsible for the success of our associates. At times, that love will be reflected in a sensitivity to an associate's anxiety; at other times, it will require high standards and expectations to focus an associate on achievement; at other times, it will mean reinforcing a successful action; and at other times, it will mean disciplining a serious misstep. All of these efforts will require more than just a mechanical effort. They require that extra measure of emotional sensitivity that is embodied in the concept of agape. *Only* when you love your associates can you perform these responsibilities with the sensitivity, compassion, and firmness required to assure successful goal achievement.

The Concept of Tough Love

The concept of "tough love" is very similar. It essentially means that parents need to love their children so much that they are able to be firm in their discipline process—to be tough, but with love. In the same way, as leaders we must care so much (love) that we are able to reinforce the required behavior through the tough discipline essential to the development of our staff. Love does not need to be soft to be real.

Remember, the objective here is the achievement of goals by your associates. Indeed, not just achievement but peak performance. That means you must lead them to success by helping them incorporate behaviors that will get results. You are the most powerful force in the lives of your associates. If you accept that heavy responsibility, then remember that your love of them will be the best guide for your actions. It will help you to make tough choices between concern for your organization's goals and concern for an associate. There is no greater challenge than to maintain that balance. Warren Bennis said it very well: "Ultimately, a leader's ability to galvanize his coworkers resides both in his understanding of himself and in his understanding of his coworker's needs and wants..."[3]

Keep in mind that few people want to fail. Failure is generally the result of misdirected effort by well-intentioned people. A leader's responsibility is to help all associates direct their efforts toward a successful result, rather than wasting their efforts on failure. The best way to accomplish that is to help associates find the answers within themselves. When you order them to act as you direct, you show them success. When you help them to discover their own potential, you show them how to succeed. This commitment is possible only if you have the capacity to love them as human beings who have a right to the dignity that comes from personal achievement.

If You Can't Love, Quit Trying to Be a Leader!

Now the real challenge: should you be a leader? If you look in the mirror and find that you cannot have agape for your associates, then you should stop trying to be a leader. If you conclude that you would rather do it yourself than have the patience that love requires to help others succeed, then quit your job as a leader. If you enjoy your own successful achievement of a task more than helping another succeed at the same task, then leave your current leadership position and get back to doing the task yourself. If you try to fake love, you will be caught. If you try to lead without love, you will fail.

As a leader, you are not alone. If your interest is in being able to do and say whatever you feel, then being a leader is the wrong role for you. You must recognize the impact that you can have on your associates. As Beverly Potter says, "Your own behavior has an impact around you. Things you do and say (or don't do and don't say) can function as antecedents that evoke—or as consequences that maintain—the behavior of someone else. The more you understand the interrelationships between your behaviors and the behaviors of subordinates, the more you can manage others by managing yourself."[4]

If, on the other hand, you're capable of agape, then you may be ready to become a good leader. True leaders have a greater joy in seeing others succeed than in experiencing their own personal achievement. They enjoy helping others triumph over major obstacles; they love seeing their associates receive awards for success; they get chills when they see a previously unsuccessful associate achieve greatness. Great leaders, like most people, have egos. But their egos are fed by the thrill of having somebody tell them they have done a great job helping somebody else succeed. If that describes you, you are the right person to lead and the rest of this book is designed to help you channel that love into those actions that will make you a great leader.

Self-Love Gives Us Strength and Confidence

The first core leadership principle is that a leader must focus on loving the associates, but if you are to accomplish that, then you must begin with a focus on loving yourself.

Loving ourselves in a healthy way creates a sense of peace with who we are. We know our strengths and weaknesses, our good qualities, and our faults, and we accept them. Indeed, our self-love allows us to forgive ourselves for our failings and allows us to reconcile those failings with our achievements. We are in balance because we are able to look past our human characteristics and accept ourselves as we are. Consider John Gardner's advice on how to renew yourself: "For self-renewing men and women the development of their own potentials and the process of self-discovery never end. It is a sad but unarguable fact that most people go through their lives only partially aware of the full range of their abilities."[5]

This love of self must not be confused with arrogance or conceit. Self-love allows us to recognize our human frailty and the need to constantly attempt to improve. At the same time, it allows us to accept our self as we find it. This self-acceptance allows us to be at peace with our existence and allows us to avoid the terrible pitfalls of self-pity, self-anger, and other self-inflicted wounds that invariably impact the way we relate to the rest of the world. For example, if you compare your knowledge, skills, and capabilities to others', you are likely to find an associate who outshines you in one or all of those categories. If you do not love yourself, you will probably be angry at yourself for being less capable than the individual you used as a benchmark comparison. That anger will eat away at your own self-concept and, in all likelihood, will be directed at the benchmark individual. Hence, not loving yourself can ultimately cause you to be unable to love your associates.

After considering whether you love yourself, you must ask whether your associates love you. Put yourself in their shoes and ask the question "If I were my leader, would I love the leader?" That takes a bit of objectivity and a great deal of honest, candid thinking on your part. Take the last week's worth of interactions with your team members and try to think through how you would have reacted to a boss who did what you did. Did you empathize at the right time? Did you criticize without constructive purpose? Did you listen to a complaint and then help the associate? Did you set an example in a time of crisis? Did you back off when you were wrong, or did you continue to try to prove you were right? In short, do you like the boss you see when you look in the mirror?

Of course, you can also go to your associates and attempt to determine directly from them how they feel. Such a poll can be very difficult to do on your own, but many organizations do climate or employee surveys with the objective of gaining a greater understanding of how leaders stand with their associates. You probably have experienced one of these in the past. How did you feel about it? Many bosses resist the results; however, they do so at their own peril. Sometimes, these kinds of surveys are the only effective way to get associates to tell you what they think you do not want to hear. Do not let self-absorption blind you from the truth of your associates' feedback.

If you are lucky, your organization has a 360-degree appraisal system where peers and subordinates get the opportunity to give you feedback. If so, treat this as an opportunity, not as a threat. You will be able to learn a great deal about how people perceive you.

LEADERSHIP TIP
Do You Really Love Yourself?

Since we are not therapists, and since self-diagnosis is very difficult, what can we do to determine if we are comfortable with ourselves? Here are some questions you might want to ask yourself. The answers are yours. There are no right answers, no wrong answers.

- When you get up in the morning, are you reluctant to go to work and deal with your associates?
- When you start a conversation with your boss, are you uneasy? Do you look forward to the meeting, or do you put it off until the last minute?
- Do you dislike the feeling you have when your boss challenges an action you have taken?
- When an associate challenges your judgment, do you get defensive and argue with that person even if you know you were wrong?
- When you and your spouse or significant other are out dining and another man or woman looks with interest, does anxiety and even anger well up inside?
- When you look in the mirror, do you dislike what you see?
- When somebody gives you a compliment, do you have a hard time saying thank you?
- Are you jealous of anybody in your family? A friend?
- Do you have trouble being alone?

If you answered "yes" to a majority of these questions, you may love yourself less than you should in order to be an effective leader. You may need help feeling better about you!

Case Study:

Patricia had a bad night, and the morning was starting off even worse. She was not only late for work, but she dreaded her upcoming meeting with her boss at 10 a.m. She knew he was going to criticize her for being behind on her project. Her staff had failed her for months now, but she had yet to figure out what to do to get the project back on track.

Frank, her favorite project leader, fell far behind, and the turnover in his group was terrible. Frank was trying everything but was having no luck with his staff. June, Patricia's least favorite manager, was continuing to annoy her. Every time she tried to get June to take on just a little more responsibility to help Frank complete his project goals, June would respond with negative, complaining feedback. She made statements like, "I am already working sixty hours a week, and I simply cannot handle any more. Why don't you figure out why Frank can't keep up?"

"How dare she try to tell me what I should do?" Patricia then would think to herself, "She has no idea the challenges that Frank has with his project. I am sick of her whining."

Patricia was fed up with the entire project and with managing a bunch of incompetent, lazy people. She thought, "Maybe I ought to fire the entire lot, except for Frank, and start all over. Maybe with a new group of people, I could find at least a couple with the smarts and the drive to get quality work done." Then she thought, "That may be the only way I am going to get my boss off my back also. If I just get rid of these people in my group, maybe my boss will give me a little more time. I'll bet I can buy at least three more weeks if I look like I am being decisive."

Patricia left work that night feeling very good. She went out with a group of friends from work, and they all told her they thought she was in trouble with her boss. To them the solution was easy: just get back on schedule. Patricia did not share with them her own strategy. She was convinced they would tell her she was being too tough, but there was no doubt in her mind she needed to get rid of the people she did not like and build a loyal staff of people just like Frank.

After carrying out the tough action she planned, Patricia felt great about her position in the company. She knew it was only a matter of time before her new staff would bail her out of the project. However, when she told her boss what she had done, he clearly was not happy with her decision. Pat was fired that same afternoon.

Where did Patricia go wrong?

Patricia's loyalty to Frank, despite his poor performance, was based on the fact that she liked him. Although we don't know her reasons, Patricia didn't like June, a good performer. The root of Patricia's problems is leader "like bias." If she had loved her project leader, she would have had an unbiased view of her team based on their individual performances. She would have seen that Frank was failing, most likely well before it became a crisis.

Making excuses for Frank, and asking others to pick up the slack for him, was absolutely the wrong thing for Patricia to do. In her capacity as leader, it was Patricia's responsibility to talk with Frank about the fact he wasn't meeting expectations and to find ways in which she could help him improve his performance. June was right on target when she asked Patricia, "Why don't you figure out why Frank can't keep up?" Clearly Patricia's "like bias" prevented her from performing as an effective leader. She failed Frank, June, and the entire team because she didn't love them. Until Patricia learns to overcome her biases and truly love each one of her associates, she should not be a leader because she will continue to fail.

(ENDNOTES)

1   John C. Maxwell, (Nashville: Thomas Nelson, 1998), 101.

2   Allan J. Cox, (New York: Dodd, Meade, 1985), 12.

3   Warren G. Bennis, (Reading: Addison-Wesley, 1989), 163.

4   Beverly A. Potter, (New York: American Management Associations Publications Group, 1980), 67.

5   John W. Gardner, (New York: W.W. Norton, 1995), 10.

CPSIA information can be obtained at www.ICGtesting.com
Printed in the USA
LVOW130716110213

319506LV00003B/11/P